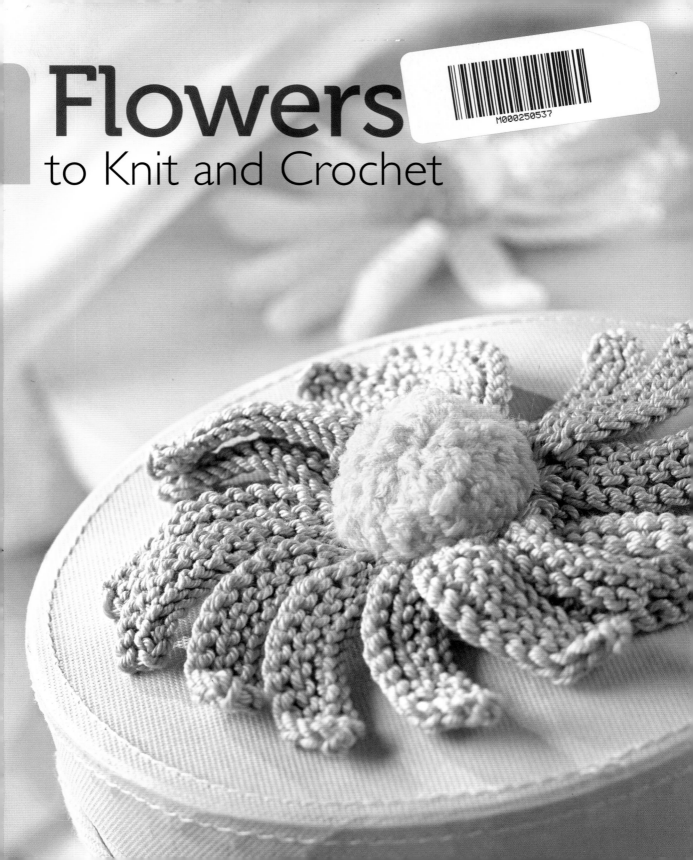

Flowers
to Knit and Crochet

First published in 2014

Search Press Limited
Wellwood, North Farm Road,
Tunbridge Wells, Kent TN2 3DR

Based on material previously published by Search Press in the
20 to Make series as *Knitted Flowers*, 2010 by Susie Johns;
and *Crocheted Flowers* by Jan Ollis, 2012

Text copyright © Susie Johns, 2010 and Jan Ollis, 2012

Photographs by Roddy Paine Photographic Studios and by
Debbie Patterson at Search Press studios

Photographs and design copyright © Search Press Ltd 2014

ISBN: 978-1-78221-051-1

Suppliers

If you have difficulty in obtaining any of the materials and
equipment mentioned in this book, then please visit the Search
Press website for details of suppliers: www.searchpress.com

Printed in China

Flowers
to Knit and Crochet

Susie Johns and Jan Ollis

Search Press

Contents

Knitted Flowers 6

Crocheted Flowers 66

Knitted Flowers

by Susie Johns

Cunningly crafted yet surprisingly quick and easy to make, this colourful collection of flowers is just the thing to use up oddments of yarn. Use them to decorate hats, hairbands, scarves, jackets, coats or cardigans; pin or stitch them to a bag, or use them to decorate household items such as cushions and tea cosies.

Whether you are a novice knitter, daunted by difficult patterns or a veteran who is eager to take a break from bigger projects, there is plenty here to occupy fidgety fingers.

Knitters have a tendency to accumulate yarn – leftovers from larger projects, sale purchases, donations or swaps – and if you search your stash you will no doubt find enough oddments to make a start. Then next time you go shopping, treat yourself to a ball of green double knitting for some stems and perhaps some yellow bouclé or an eye-catching eyelash yarn for a bold centre or some sensational stamens. Tapestry yarns and novelty embroidery threads can also be introduced.

On a technical note, unless otherwise stated, right and wrong sides of work are interchangeable: just decide which side of the flower or petal looks best, or base your decision on which way the petals curl. Tension (or gauge) is not given: just aim for a firm fabric that will hold its shape, using a smaller needle than the one stated in the pattern, if necessary, to produce the right result.

Some of the patterns, such as the Arum Lily, require you to knit in the round on double-pointed needles, so if you find the idea too challenging, start with one of the easier projects such as the Cosmos, Daisy, Tulip, Anemone or Cactus Flower. If you prefer a challenge, however, then head straight for the Periwinkle and Sweet William – though the seasoned knitter will find these simple, I am sure.

The flowers

Water Lily, page 10

Zinnia, page 12

Cactus Flower, page 14

Pansy, page 16

Daffodil, page 18

Peace Lily, page 20

Grape Hyacinth, page 22

Cosmos, page 24

Hibiscus, page 26

Clematis, page 28

Sweet William, page 30

Red Poppy, page 32

Chrysanthemum, page 34

Tulip, page 36

Periwinkle, page 38

Anemone, page 40

Cherry Blossom, page 42

Arum Lily, page 44

Daisy, page 46

Rose, page 48

Snowdrop, page 50

Viola, page 52

Passionflower, page 54

Pelargonium, page 56

Peony, page 58

Lavender, page 60

Crocus, page 62

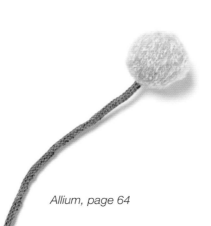

Allium, page 64

Water Lily

Instructions:

Outer flower

Cast on 9 sts.

Row 1: k all sts tbl.

Row 2: k.

Row 3: inc 1, k to end (10 sts).

Row 4: k.

Row 5: inc 1, k to end (11 sts).

Row 6: k.

Row 7: inc 1, k to end (12 sts).

Row 8: k.

Row 9: k2tog, k to end (11 sts).

Row 10: k.

Row 11: k2tog, k to end (10 sts).

Row 12: k.

Row 13: k2tog, k to end (9 sts).

Row 14: k.

Row 15: cast off 6, k to end.

Row 16: k3, cast on 6 (8 sts).

Rep rows 1–16 three times more and rows 1–14 once, then cast off all sts; break yarn and fasten off.

Inner flower

Cast on 8 sts.

Row 1: k all sts tbl.

Row 2: k.

Row 3: inc 1, k to end (9 sts).

Row 4: k.

Row 5: inc 1, k to end (10 sts).

Next 3 rows: k.

Row 9: k2tog, k to end (9 sts).

Row 10: k.

Row 11: k2tog, k to end (8 sts).

Row 12: k.

Row 13: cast off 5, k to end.

Row 14: k3, cast on 5 (8 sts).

Rep rows 1–14 twice more and rows 1–12 once, then cast off all sts; break yarn and fasten off.

Centre

Cast on 6 sts.

Row 1: cast off 5 sts, turn.

Row 2: cast on 5 sts.

Rep rows 1 and 2 seven times more, then cast off all sts; break yarn and fasten off.

Making up

Join the two ends of the outer flower by stitching the lower corners of the two end petals together, then run a thread along the base of all the petals and pull up tightly to gather; do the same with the inner flower and the flower centre. Stitch the inner flower on top of the outer flower, matching centres. Stitch the flower centre in place.

Materials:

Double knitting yarn, bright pink

Polyester double knitting yarn, bright yellow

Needles:

1 pair 3.00mm (UK 11; US 2) knitting needles

Tapestry needle

Measurements:

Finished flower measures 12cm (4¾in) across

The deep
pink water lily
could make
a big, bold
corsage to wear on
a winter coat or a
felt hat or beret. To knit the pale pink
alternative, make up the flower using
a textured pale pink yarn and make
the flower centre with an acid yellow
mohair yarn for a textural contrast.

Zinnia

Instructions:

Petals (in one piece)

With two strands of main yarn and 2.75mm (UK 12; US 2) needles, cast on 12 sts.

Row 1: k all sts tbl.

Row 2: k.

Row 3: inc 1, k to end (13 sts).

Row 4: k.

Row 5: inc 1, k to end (14 sts).

Row 6: k.

Row 7: k2tog, k to end (13 sts).

Row 8: k.

Row 9: k2tog, k to end (12 sts).

Row 10: k.

Row 11: k2tog, k to end 11 sts).

Row 12: k.

Row 13: cast off 10, turn.

Row 14: cast on 11 (12 sts).

Rep rows 1–14 four times more and rows 1–14 once, then cast off all sts; break yarn and fasten off.

Centre

With eyelash yarn and 2.75mm needles, cast on 12 sts and work 20 rows in garter stitch (k every row), then cast off; break yarn and fasten off.

Making up

Bring the two edges of the knitting together to make a circle of petals and stitch the lower corners of the two end petals together. Run a gathering stitch around the centre, along the base of each petal and pull up tightly to gather.

Run a gathering stitch all round the edge of the centre, place the button inside and pull up tightly to gather up and enclose the button. Stitch the flower centre firmly in place.

With small, sharp scissors, trim away strands of yarn from the top surface of the flower centre, close to the knitted stitches (be careful not to cut the stitches), leaving strands radiating out from the sides only.

Materials:

Mohair yarn, yellow-green

Eyelash yarn, rainbow

Round button, 23mm ($^7/_8$in)

Small, sharp scissors

Needles:

1 pair 2.75mm (UK 12; US 2) knitting needles

Tapestry needle

Measurements:

Finished flower measures 14.5cm (5¾in) across

Note:

For knitting petals, use yarn double.

Opposite

This big, bold flower makes a great decoration for a winter coat or wrap, or to add a splash of colour to a plain cardigan. Petals knitted in a pink-violet shade of mohair yarn, with the same rainbow yarn in the centre, create a very exotic bloom.

Cactus Flower

Materials:

Pale green mohair yarn

Polyester double knitting yarn, bright yellow

Pure wool double knitting yarn, brown

Novelty chenille thread, bright pink

Flower pot, 10cm (4in) in diameter

Scrap of stiff card

Polyester wadding or toy stuffing

Fabric glue or all-purpose adhesive (optional)

Needles:

Set of 5 double-pointed knitting needles, 3.00mm (UK 11; US 2)

1 pair 2.25mm (UK 13; US 1) knitting needles

Tapestry needle

Measurements:

Finished flower measures 6cm (2³⁄₈in) across and cactus measures 8cm (3¹⁄₈in) high

Instructions:

Cactus

With mohair yarn and size 3.00mm (UK 11; US 2) double-pointed needles, cast on 8 sts and distribute between four needles.

Round 1: k.

Round 2: inc in each st (16 sts).

Round 3: (inc 1, k3) 4 times (20 sts).

Round 4: (inc 1, k4) 4 times (24 sts).

Round 5: (inc 1, k5) 4 times (28 sts).

Round 5: (inc 1, k6) 4 times (32 sts).

Knit 15 rounds without further increases.

Round 21: (k2tog, k6) 4 times (28 sts).

Knit 5 rounds.

Round 27: (k2tog, k5) 4 times (24 sts).

Knit 9 rounds.

Cast off; break yarn and fasten off.

Flower (in one piece)

With yellow yarn and size 2.25mm (UK 13; US 1) needles, cast on 9 sts.

Row 1: k all sts tbl.

Row 2: p6, turn.

Row 3: k to end.

Row 4: p.

Row 5: cast off 7 sts knitwise, k rem st.

Row 6: k2, cast on 7 sts.

Rep rows 1–6 four times more, then rep rows 1–4 once; cast off all sts knitwise; break yarn and fasten off.

Earth

With brown DK yarn used double and two size 3.00mm needles, cast on 8 sts.

Row 1: k.

Row 2: inc 1, k to end.

Rep last row until there are 20 sts.

Knit 8 rows without further increases.

Cast off 1 st at beg of next 12 rows.

Cast off rem 8 sts; break yarn and fasten off.

Making up

Cut a circle of stiff card 9cm (3½in) in diameter. Stitch a gathering thread all round the edge of the brown piece of knitting (earth), place the card circle centrally on the wrong side and pull up thread to gather; fasten off.

Stuff the cactus firmly with polyester wadding. Using matching green yarn, stitch the base of the cactus to the earth.

Bring the two edges of the flower petals together to make a circle and stitch the lower corners of the two end petals together; then run a gathering stitch along the base of the petals and pull up tightly to gather. Stitch a few strands of pink chenille thread in the centre of the flower, then stitch the flower in place on top of the cactus. Finally, wedge the whole thing into the top of a flower pot or small ornamental bucket; glue in place if you wish.

These exotic novelty knits are great for decorating windowsills, whatever the season. For the alternative cactus, use an emerald green linen slub yarn and make up the flower in a red pure wool double knitting yarn with a centre made from rainbow eyelash yarn.

Pansy

Instructions:

Plain petal

With violet yarn and size 3.00mm (UK 11; US 2) needles, cast on 5 sts.

Row 1: inc in each st to end (10 sts).

Row 2: k.

Row 3: inc in each st to end (20 sts).

Row 4: k.

Row 5: inc in each st to end (40 sts).

Knit 3 rows.

Cast off; break yarn and fasten off.

Two-colour petal

With pink-violet yarn and 3.00mm needles, cast on 5 sts and work rows 1 to 3; break yarn.

Join in violet yarn and work pattern from row 4 to end.

Three-colour petal

With yellow yarn and 3.00mm needles, cast on 5 sts and work row 1; break yarn.

Join in violet-pink yarn and work rows 2 and 3; break yarn.

Join in violet yarn and work pattern from row 4 to end.

Making up

Fold each petal in half with right sides together and stitch cast-on edge and sides to form a central seam.

Place the two three-colour petals right sides together and stitch two edges together. Open out.

Place the two two-colour petals on top, overlapping slightly, and stitch in place.

Place the plain petal behind the other petals to form the top of the flower and stitch in place.

Finally, with spare yellow yarn, embroider 4 chain stitches from centre to base of each three-colour petal and a few straight stitches in the centre of the flower.

Materials:

Pure wool double knitting yarn, violet, pink-violet and yellow

Needles:

1 pair 3.00mm (UK 11; US 2) knitting needles

Tapestry needle

Measurements:

Finished flower measures 11cm (4³/₈in) across

Opposite

Stitch your knitted pansies to an old-fashioned tea cosy for a touch of nostalgia, or to the ends of a scarf, or make a brooch to decorate your knitwear. Experiment with other colour combinations, such as pink-violet petals with claret centres and the same yellow detail as the main flower. In the background flower here, the 'wrong' sides of the petals have been used, creating a slightly different effect.

Daffodil

Instructions:

Trumpet

With 3.00mm (UK 11; US 2) needles and yarn A, cast on 4 sts.

Row 1 (WS): purl.

Row 2: (inc 1 in each stitch) 4 times (8 sts).

Row 3: purl.

Row 4: (inc 1 in each stitch) 8 times (16 sts)

Row 5: purl.

Row 6: (inc 1 in next stitch) k3 4 times (20 sts).

Row 7: purl.

Row 8: (inc 1 in next stitch), k4 4 times (24 sts).

Beg with a purl row, work 15 rows in stocking stitch.

Row 23: (inc 1 in each stitch) 24 times (48 sts).

Cast-off row: cast off 1 st, *transfer stitch from right-hand to left-hand needle, cast on 1 st, cast off 3 sts; rep from * to end.

Cut yarn and fasten off.

Petal (make 6)

With same needles and yarn A, cast on 4 sts.

Row 1: p3, inc 2 knitwise, p3 (9 sts).

Row 2: k3, p3, k3.

Row 3: p3. inc 1 knitwise, k1, inc 1 knitwise, p3 (11 sts).

Row 4: k3, p5, k3.

Row 5: p3, k5, p3.

Row 6: k3, p5, k3.

Row 7: p3, inc 1. knitwise, k3, inc 1 knitwise, p3 (13 sts).

Row 8: k3, p7, k3.

Row 9: p3, k7, p3.

Rows 10–12: rep rows 8 and 9 once then row 8 once more.

Row 13: p3, inc 1 knitwise, k5, inc 1 knitwise, p3 (15 sts).

Row 14: k3, p9, k3.

Row 15: p3, k9, p3.

Rows 16–18: rep rows 14 and 15 once then row 14 once more.

Row 19: p3, k2tog tbl, k5, k2tog, p3 (13 sts).

Row 20: k3, p7, k3.

Row 21: p3, k2tog tbl, k3, k2tog, p3 (11 sts).

Row 22: k3, p5, k3.

Row 23: p3, k2tog tbl, k1, k2tog, p3 (9 sts).

Row 24: k3, p3, k3.

Row 25: p3, sl1 purlwise with yarn at back, k2tog, psso, p3 (7 sts).

Row 26: k3, p1, k3.

Row 27: p2, p3tog, p2 (5 sts).

Row 28: knit.

Row 29: p1, p3tog, p1 (3 sts).

Row 30: knit.

Row 31: cut yarn and fasten off.

Materials:

Lightweight DK yarn, yellow (A) and green (B)

DK wool yarn, green

Pipe cleaner, 28cm (11in)

Needles:

1 pair 3.00mm (UK 11; US 2) knitting needles

Tapestry needle

Measurements:

Finished flower 37cm (14½in) long, including stalk; each petal is 8cm (3¼in) long and 4cm (1½in) wide.

Stalk

With 3.00mm (UK 11; US 2) needles and yarn B, cast on 85 sts.

Work 5 rows in stocking stitch.

Cast off.

Leaf

With 3.00mm (UK 11; US 2) needles and yarn B, cast on 5 sts.

Beg with a knit row, work 20 rows in stocking stitch.

Row 21: (inc 1 in first stitch), k3, inc 1 in last stitch (7 sts).

Row 22: k2, p3, k2.

Row 23: knit.

Rep rows 22 and 23 thirty times.

Row 84: k2tog, k1, p1, k1, k2tog (5 sts).

Row 85: knit.

Row 86: k2tog, k1, k2tog (3 sts).

Row 87: sl1, k2tog, psso.

Cut yarn and fasten off.

Making up

Stitch the lower corners of the petals together so that petals form a ring. Run a gathering stitch around the base of the petals and pull up slightly, so that the base of the trumpet fits inside. Stitch the side seam on the trumpet, then stitch the trumpet in place. To make the stalk, wrap the strip of knitting round a pipe cleaner and stitch cast-on and cast-off edges together. Stitch the top of the stalk to the base of the trumpet. Stitch the leaf in place, positioning the base of the leaf about 7cm (2¾in) from the bottom of the stem.

These daffodils make lovely decorations for Easter, or just for spring. You could drape a single daffodil across the top of a mirror or picture frame, or make a bunch to place in a vase.

Peace Lily

Instructions:

With white yarn and size 3.00mm (UK 11; US 2) needles, cast on 9 sts.

Row 1: k.

Row 2: k1, p7, k1.

Row 3: k1, (inc 1, k1) 4 times (13 sts).

Row 4: k1, p11, k1.

Row 5: k1, (inc 1, k1) 6 times, k1 (19 sts).

Row 6: k1, p17, k1.

Row 7: k1, (inc 1) 17 times, k1 (35 sts).

Row 8: k1, p33, k1.

Row 9: k.

Rep rows 8 and 9 three times.

Rep row 8 once.

Row 17: (k2, k2tog) 4 times, k4, (sl 1, k1, psso, k2) 4 times (28 sts).

Row 18: k1, p26, k1.

Row 19: (k2, k2tog) 3 times, k4 (sl 1, k1, psso, k2) 3 times (22 sts).

Row 20: k1, p20, k1.

Row 21: (k2, k2tog) twice, k6, (sl 1, k1, psso, k2) twice (18 sts).

Row 22: k1, p16, k1.

Row 23: (k2, k2tog) twice, k2, (sl 1, k1, psso, k2) twice (14 sts).

Row 24: k1, p12, k1.

Row 25: k2, k2tog, k2tog, sl 1, k1, psso, k2tog, sl 1, k1, psso, k2 (9 sts).

Row 26: k1, p7, k1.

Row 27: k1, k2tog, sl 1, k1, psso, k1, sl 1, k1, psso, k1 (6 sts).

Row 28: k1, p2tog tbl, p2tog, k1 (4 sts).

Row 29: k1, sl 2, k1, psso (2 sts).

Row 30: p2tog; break yarn and fasten off.

Spadix

With yellow bouclé yarn and size 3.00mm needles, cast on 16 sts, knit 5 rows and cast off; break yarn and fasten off.

Stem

With green yarn and two double-pointed needles, cast on 5 sts.

Row 1: k5; do not turn but slide sts to other end of needle.

Rep this row until work measures 7cm (2¾in); fasten off.

Making up

To form the spadix, fold under 1.5cm (¾in) at one end, then slip stitch the long edges together to make a firm tube. Stitch the narrower end to the top of the stem. Place inside the flower, positioning the join at the base of the flower and stitch, wrapping the cast-on edge around to hide the join.

Materials:

Cotton/acrylic double knitting yarn, white

Acrylic double knitting bouclé yarn, yellow

Pure wool double knitting yarn, green

Needles:

1 pair 3.00mm (UK 11; US 2) knitting needles

2 double-pointed 3.00mm (UK 11; US 2) knitting needles

Tapestry needle

Measurements:

Finished flower is 15cm (6in) long, including stem

Pin or stitch the lily to a bag
or purse, or a jacket lapel.
Instead of white, you could
knit the main part of the
flower in a deep coral pink
cotton double knitting yarn.

Grape Hyacinth

Instructions:

To make a bobble (mb)
Knit into front, back and front of stitch, turn; k3, turn; k3, turn; pass 2nd and 3rd stitches over 1st stitch, then slip this stitch back on to right-hand needle; turn.

Flower
With silk yarn and 3.25mm (UK 10; US 3) needles, cast on 15 sts.

Row 1: *mb, k3, rep from * to end.

Row 2: p.

Row 3: k2, (mb, k3) 4 times, k1.

Row 4: p .

Rep rows 1–4 once, then rep rows 1 and 2 once; cast off all sts knitwise; break yarn and fasten off.

Stem
With green yarn and two double-pointed needles, cast on 2 sts.

Row 1: k2; do not turn but slide sts to other end of needle.

Rep this row until work measures 6.5cm (2½in); fasten off.

Making up
Place the cast-off edge of the flower over the cast-on edge, overlapping slightly, and slip stitch it in place. Stitch the three bobbles at the top of the flower in a cluster. Insert the end of the stem into the base of the flower and stitch it in place.

Materials:

Chinese silk yarn, bright purple

Pure wool double knitting yarn, green

Needles:

1 pair 3.25mm (UK 10; US 3) knitting needles,

2 double-pointed 3.00mm (UK 11; US 2) knitting needles

Tapestry needle

Measurements:

Finished flower is 14.5cm (5¾in) long, including stem

To make a lapel pin, use matching yarn to stitch a brooch pin to the slip-stitched seam.

Hyacinths could be used singly or in a bunch, as a lapel pin on a jacket. Use a textured, variegated yarn in pink/purple for an alternative; if it is slightly thicker, the resulting flower will be larger, even if you use the same size needles.

Cosmos

Instructions:

Petal (make 8)

With deep pink yarn and size 2.75mm (UK 12; US 2) needles, cast on 2 sts.

Knit 2 rows.

Row 3: (inc 1) twice (4 sts).

Knit 5 rows.

Next row: k1, (inc 1) twice, k1 (6 sts).

Knit 5 rows.

Next row: k1, (k2tog) twice, k1 (4 sts).

Knit 2 rows.

Cast off, break yarn and fasten off.

Centre

With yellow yarn and 2.75mm needles, cast on 2 sts.

Row 1: inc 1, k to end.

Rep last row until there are 8 sts.

Knit 3 rows.

Next row: cast off 1, k to end.

Rep last row until there are 2 sts.

Cast off; break yarn and fasten off.

Making up

Placing the cast-off ends in the centre, stitch the petals edge to edge.

With red tapestry yarn, stitch a long, straight stitch in the centre of each flower petal, radiating out from the middle of the flower.

Run a gathering stitch all round the edge of the centre piece, place the button inside and pull up tightly to gather up and enclose the button.

Stitch the flower centre firmly in place.

Opposite

To brighten up the house, stitch flowers to cushions, curtain tie-backs or place mats. Choose bright coloured yarn for the main part of the flower. The variation shown here is orange but you could make up flowers in red, yellow, purple and white, too.

Materials:

Lightweight pure wool double knitting yarn, deep pink and yellow

Tapestry wool, red

Round button, 12mm (½in)

Needles:

1 pair 2.75mm (UK 12; US 2) knitting needles

Tapestry needle

Measurements:

Finished flower measures 9cm (3½in) across

Hibiscus

Instructions:

With salmon pink yarn and size 3.00mm (UK 11; US 2) needles, cast on 4 sts.

Row 1: inc 1, k to end.

Row 2: inc 1, p to end.

Rep rows 1 and 2 twice more (10 sts).

Row 7: sl 1, k to end.

Row 8: sl 1 knitwise, p to last st, k1.

Rep rows 7 and 8 twice more.

Cut yarn, slip to base of left-hand needle or transfer to spare needle.

Make 4 more petals in the same way; do not break yarn on last petal.

Next row: k to end, knit across all sts of 4 reserved petals (50 sts).

Next row: p; break yarn.

Next row: join in red yarn * k2tog, rep from * to end (25 sts).

Next row: p.

Next row: * k2tog, rep from * to last st, k1 (13 sts).

Next row: * p2tog, rep from * to last st, p1.

Cut yarn, leaving a tail and thread this through rem 7 sts.

Pistil

With orange yarn and two double-pointed needles, cast on 2 sts.

Row 1: k2; do not turn but slide sts to other end of needle.

Rep this row until work measures 3 cm (1¼in); break off yarn and join in yellow.

Next row: k.

Next row: inc in each st (4 sts).

Next row: inc 1, k to end (5 sts).

Rep last row once more.

Next row: k.

Next row: cast off 1, k to end.

Rep last row until there are 2 sts.

Cast off; break yarn, leaving a tail.

Making up

Bring the two edges of the flower petals together, stitch the lower parts of the two end petals together; then run a gathering stitch along the base of the petals and pull up tightly to gather, trapping the base of the pistil in the centre. Stitch securely in place. Fold over the yellow part of the pistil and stitch to form a neat bobble.

Materials:

4-ply wool or wool-blend yarn, deep salmon pink and red

Tapestry wool, orange

Acrylic double knitting bouclé yarn, yellow

Needles:

1 pair 3.00mm (UK 11; US 2) knitting needles,

Tapestry needle

Measurements:

Finished flower measures 11cm (4³/₈in) across

Opposite

Stitch a hibiscus to the ends of a silk scarf, pin to the lapel of a jacket, or use to decorate a hat for a special occasion. The alternative has been made using a bamboo yarn in subtle shades of peach and apricot. The pistil is made in the same apricot yarn. Using this different yarn type but the same needles, the flower ends up slightly larger, measuring 13cm (5¹/₈in) at its widest point.

Clematis

Instructions:

Petal (make 8)

With deep violet yarn and size 3.00mm (UK 11; US 2) needles, cast on 7 sts.

Row 1 (WS): p3, inc 1, p3 (9 sts).

Row 2: k3, p3, k3.

Row 3: p3, inc 1, k1, inc 1, p3 (11 sts).

Row 4: k3, p5, k3.

Row 5: p3, k5, p3.

Rep rows 4 and 5 once more.

Row 8: as row 4.

Row 9: p3, k1, sl1, k2tog, psso, k1, p3 (9 sts).

Row 10: k3, p3, k3.

Row 11: p3, sl1, k2tog, psso, p3 (7 sts).

Row 12: k3, p1, k3.

Row 13: p2, p3tog, p2 (5 sts).

Row 14: k.

Row 15: p1, p3tog, p1 (3 sts).

Row 16: k.

Row 17: p3tog; break yarn and fasten off.

Making up

Join four petals together at the corners, using tails of yarn. Thread a long tail of yarn in a running stitch through the base of each petal, then pull up the thread to gather tightly. Fasten off. Repeat with the other four petals. Place one group of four on top of the other and stitch them together.

To make the centre, wind eyelash yarn around two fingers about twelve times. Tie yarn around the centre to form a small bundle, then pull the ends through the flower centre and secure. Trim with scissors.

Opposite

Make a statement by pinning one or more clematis to a hatband, or use to decorate a bag or purse. The alternative here has been made up in a very pale pink bamboo yarn; the same yarn has been used to make a frayed flower centre.

Materials:

Felting yarn, pure wool, deep violet

Eyelash yarn, 100% polyester, white

Scissors

Needles:

1 pair 3.00mm (UK 11; US 2) knitting needles

Tapestry needle

Measurements:

Finished flower measures 14cm (5½in) across

Sweet William

Instructions:

With white yarn and size 3.00mm (UK 11; US 2) double-pointed needles, cast on 10 sts and distribute between four needles as follows: four on one needle and two each on the other three needles.

Round 1: k; cut yarn.

Round 2: join in red yarn and k1 round.

Round 3: inc in every stitch (20 sts).

Round 4: inc in every stitch (50 sts); cut yarn.

Row 5: join in pink yarn, k 8, turn.

Next row: k.

Cast off; cut yarn and fasten off.

Rejoin yarn to next st in round and rep from Row 5 four times more.

Making up

Weave in red and white yarn ends on the wrong side of the flower.

Run each pink yarn end down the side of the petal, neatening the petal edges as you do this, and fasten at the back of the work.

Opposite

This tiny flower makes a lovely brooch. You could also stitch one or more to a hair slide or alice band for a pretty hair decoration, or attach shoe clips to decorate a plain pair of shoes, as shown here. Vary the design by using different combinations of the three colours.

Materials:

4-ply cotton yarn, red, pink and white

Needles:

Set of 5 double-pointed 3.00mm (UK 11; US 2) knitting needles

Tapestry needle

Measurements:

Finished flower measures 4.5cm (1¾in) across

Red Poppy

Instructions:

Petal (make 4)

With red chunky yarn and size 3.25mm (UK 10; US 3) needles, cast on 13 sts.

Row 1: k all sts tbl.

Row 2: sl 1, k11, turn, leaving rem stitches on needle.

Row 3: k11, turn.

Rep row 3 seven more times.

Row 11: k10, k2tog.

Row 12: sl1, k9, k2tog.

Row 13: k to end.

Rep last row 5 times.

Row 19: k4, sl 1, k2tog, psso, k4.

Row 20: k.

Row 21: k3, sl 1, k2tog, psso, k3.

Row 22: k.

Row 23: k2, sl 1, k2tog, psso, k2.

Row 24: k.

Row 25: k1, sl 1, k2tog, psso, k1.

Row 26: sl 1, k2tog, psso; fasten off.

Centre

With black linen yarn and 2.25mm (UK 13; US 1) needles, cast on 6 sts.

Row 1: k.

Row 2: inc 1, k to last st, inc 1 (8 sts).

Row 3: inc 1, k to last st, inc 1 (10 sts).

Knit 10 rows.

Row 14: k2tog, k to last 2 sts, k2tog (8 sts).

Row 14: k2tog, k to last 2 sts, k2tog (6 sts).

Cast off.

Stamens

With black linen yarn and 2.25mm needles, cast on 10 sts.

Row 1: cast off, leaving 1 st on needle.

Row 2: cast on 9 sts.

Row 3: cast off, leaving 1 st on needle.

Rep rows 2 and 3 six times more.

Cast off rem st.

Making up

Stitch the petals together, arranging them so that the pointed bases meet in the centre and each straight side edge overlaps its neighbour by about 2mm (1/8in).

Stitch a running thread around the edge of the centre piece, place the button inside and pull up the yarn to gather; fasten off securely.

Join the two ends of the row of stamens, then run a thread along the base and pull up to gather. Stitch to the centre of the flower and stitch the covered button on top.

Materials:

Chunky acrylic yarn, red

Linen double knitting yarn, black

Round button, 22mm (8⅝in)

Needles:

1 pair 2.25mm (UK 13; US 1) knitting needles

1 pair 3.25mm (UK 10; US 3) knitting needles

Tapestry needle

Measurements:

Finished flower measures 12cm (4¾in) across

Use the red poppy as a corsage on a plain coat, or pin it to a hat to make a statement. For an alternative, use a pure wool double knitting yarn in pink, with a grey wool centre. Using a lighter yarn with the same size needles produces a slightly smaller flower (this one is 11cm/4³/₈in in diameter).

Chrysanthemum

Instructions:

With mustard yellow yarn and size 3.25mm (UK 10; US 3) needles, cast on 22 sts.

Row 1: k all sts tbl.

Row 2: k all sts tbl.

Row 3: cast off, leaving 1 st on needle.

Row 4: cast on 21 sts.

Row 5: k all sts tbl.

Rep rows 2–5 13 times more, then row 2 once.

Next row: cast on 19 sts.

Next row: k all sts tbl.

Next row: k all sts tbl.

Next row: cast off, leaving 1 st on needle.

Rep last row four times more.

Next row: cast on 15 sts.

Next row: k all sts tbl.

Next row: cast off, leaving 1 st on needle.

Rep last three rows 5 times.

Next row: cast on 12 sts.

Next row: k all sts tbl.

Next row: cast off, leaving 1 st on needle.

Rep last three rows 5 times then cast off rem st, break yarn and fasten off.

Making up

Stitch a gathering thread along the base of all the petals and pull up tightly to gather. Form some of the longer petals into loops, stitching the end of each one securely to the centre of the flower.

Materials:

Wool and cotton double knitting yarn, mustard yellow

Needles:

1 pair 3.25mm (UK 10; US 3) knitting needles

Tapestry needle

Measurements:

Finished flower measures approximately 12cm (4¾in) across

Opposite

As an alternative, use a variegated cotton double knitting yarn and, using the instructions as a guide, make only twenty-eight petals in total, six of 16 sts, twelve of 13 sts, and ten of 10 sts. When making up, do not loop any of the petals.

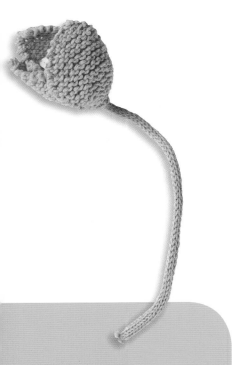

Tulip

Instructions:

Petal (make 3)

With orange yarn and 3.25mm (UK 10; US 3) needles, cast on 5 sts

Round 1: k.

Row 1: k each st tbl.

Row 2: k1, inc 1, k1, inc 1, k1 (7 sts).

Row 3: k.

Row 4: k2, inc 1, k1, inc 1, k2 (9 sts).

Row 5: k.

Row 6: k3, inc 1, k1, inc 1, k3 (11 sts).

Row 7: k.

Row 8: k4, inc 1, k1, inc 1, k4 (13 sts).

Row 9: k.

Row 10: k5, inc 1, k1, inc 1, k5 (15 sts).

Knit 8 rows.

Row 19: sl 1, k1, psso, k11, k2tog (13 sts).

Row 20: k.

Row 21: sl 1, k1, psso, k9, k2tog (11 sts).

Row 22: k.

Row 23: sl 1, k1, psso, k7, k2tog (9 sts).

Row 24: k.

Row 25: sl 1, k1, psso, k5, k2tog (7 sts).

Row 26: k.

Row 27: sl 1, k1, psso, k3, k2tog (5 sts).

Row 28: k.

Row 29: sl 1, k1, psso, k1, k2tog (3 sts).

Row 30: sl 1, k2tog, psso; fasten off.

Stalk

With green yarn and two double-pointed needles, cast on 5 sts.

Row 1: k5; do not turn but slide sts to other end of needle.

Rep this row until work measures 21cm (8¼in); fasten off.

Making up

Fold over 5mm (¼in) at either end of one of the pipe cleaners and slip it inside the stalk. Stitch the ends of the stalk closed. Stitch the top of the stalk to the base of one of the petals. Cut the second pipe cleaner into three equal lengths, fold each one in half and attach to the top of the stalk to create stamens. Wrap the two remaining petals around the first and stitch.

Materials:

Linen double knitting yarn, orange

2 yellow pipe cleaners, 23cm (9in)

Pure wool double knitting yarn, green

Needles:

1 pair 3.25mm (UK 10, US 3) knitting needles

1 pair double-pointed knitting needles, 3.00mm (UK11; US2)

Tapestry needle

Measurements:

Finished flower measures approximately 7cm (2¾in) across and 31cm (12¼in) long

*Tulips come in lots of lovely colours;
choose your favourite. Arrange single tulips
on a shelf or across the top of a mirror or
picture frame, or display in a vase.*

Periwinkle

Instructions:

Petal (make 5)

With blue yarn and size 2.25mm (UK 13; US 1) needles, cast on 12 sts.

Row 1: (k1, sl 1 purlwise with yarn at back of work) six times.

Rep last row 15 times; break off yarn.

Join in ivory yarn and rep row 1 six times more.

Break off yarn, leaving a long tail; transfer to a stitch holder.

Making up

Each petal needs to be finished off before joining to make up the flower. Thread the tail of yarn on to a tapestry needle. Carefully slip stitches off the stitch holder and pull apart the two sides of the petal, separating the stitches. Thread the yarn through each stitch in turn then turn the petal inside out and pull up the yarn to gather the base of the petal.

Join the petals at the centre, then sew on a little cluster of eight seed beads.

Materials:

Pure wool 4-ply yarn, blue and ivory

Glass seed beads, yellow

Sewing thread, white or yellow

Needles:

1 pair 2.25mm (UK 13; US 1) knitting needles

Tapestry needle

Stitch holder

Sewing needle

Measurements:

Finished flower measures 7cm (2¾in) across

Opposite

These little woollen flowers have a very retro feel. Pin them to a cardigan, a linen jacket or woolly hat. You can also make a plain blue version.

Anemone

Instructions:

Petal (make 6)

With purple yarn and size 2.75mm (UK 12; US 2) needles, cast on 4 sts.

Row 1: k all sts tbl.

Row 2: inc 1, k to end.

Rep last row until there are 10 sts.

Knit 10 rows.

Next row: k1, sl 1, k1, psso, k4, k2tog, k1.

Next row: k1, sl 1, k1, psso, k2, k2tog, k1.

Next row: k1, sl 1, k1, psso, k2tog, k1.

Next row: k2tog twice.

Next row: k2tog.

Fasten off.

Centre

With black yarn and size 2.75mm needles, cast on 2 sts.

Row 1: inc 1, k to end.

Rep row 1 until there are 6 sts.

Knit 3 rows.

Next row: cast off 1, k to end.

Rep last row until there are 2 sts.

Cast off; break yarn and fasten off.

Making up

Position the petals so that cast-off end is at the centre. Stitch the petals together, overlapping each one. Stitch a running thread around the edge of the centre piece, place the button inside and pull up the yarn to gather; fasten off securely.

Thread the tapestry needle with a length of white eyelash yarn and overstitch the perimeter of the covered button. Tease out a few of the strands. Stitch the button to the flower centre.

Materials:

Lambswool and mohair double knitting yarn, purple and black

Eyelash yarn, white

Round button, 12mm (½in)

Needles:

1 pair knitting needles, 2.75mm (UK 12; US 2)

Tapestry needle

Measurements:

Finished flower measures approximately 9cm (3½in) across

Opposite

Use the same yarn in red to make a perfect partner for the purple anemone. Pin or stitch one or more anemones to a plain sweater or scarf, or fasten to a length of ribbon to make a choker.

Cherry Blossom

Instructions:

Petal (make 5)

With pale pink yarn and size 3.00mm (UK 11; US 2) needles, cast on 5 sts.

Row 1: k4, turn, leaving rem st on needle.

Row 2: p3, turn, leaving rem st on needle.

Row 3: k3, turn.

Row 4: p3, turn.

Row 5: k4.

Row 6: p2tog, p1, p2tog (3 sts).

Row 7: k1, k2tog, psso.

Fasten off.

Making up

Join the petals at the centre, inserting stamens and securing them with a few stitches.

Opposite

The perfect choice for a bridesmaid, stitch one or more blossoms to a hair slide or clip for a pretty hair decoration, or to a length of ribbon to make a choker or wrist corsage. For an alternative, use double knitting cotton yarn in a bright pink and, instead of stamens, stitch a few seed beads in the centre of the flower.

Materials:

Bamboo double knitting yarn, very pale pink

Pearl stamens

Needles:

1 pair 3.00mm (UK 11; US 2) knitting needles

Tapestry needle

Measurements:

Finished flower measures 5cm (2in) across

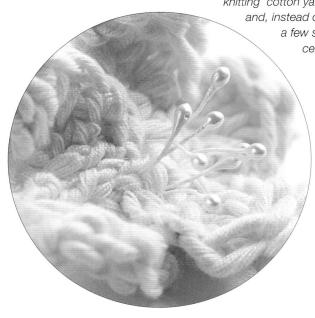

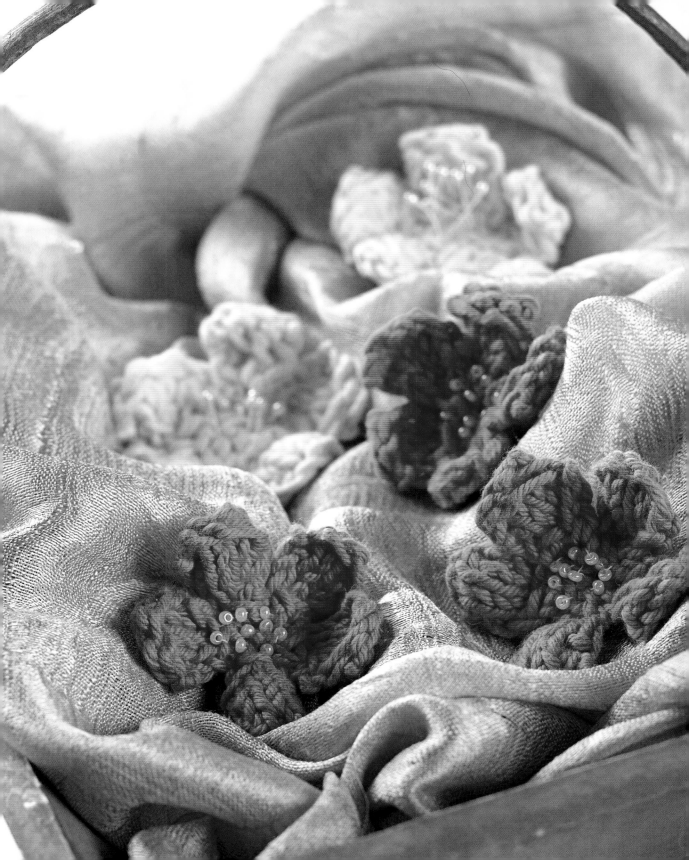

Arum Lily

Instructions:

With white yarn and size 3.00mm double-pointed needles, cast on 8 sts and distribute between four needles.

Knit 3 rounds.

Round 4: inc in each st (16 sts).

Knit 3 rounds.

Round 8: (inc 1, k3) 4 times (20 sts).

Knit 2 rounds.

Round 11: (inc 1, k4) 4 times (24 sts).

Knit 2 rounds.

Round 14: inc 1, k5) 4 times (28 sts).

Knit 2 rounds.

Round 17: (inc 1, k6) 4 times (32 sts).

Knit 8 rounds.

Round 26: (inc 1, k7) 4 times (36 sts).

Round 27: (inc 1, k8) 4 times (40 sts).

Round 28: (inc 1, k9) 4 times (44 sts).

Round 29: (inc 1, k10) 4 times (48 sts).

Round 30: (inc 1, k11) 4 times (52 sts).

Round 31: (inc 1, k12) 4 times (56 sts).

Round 32: (inc 1, k13) 4 times (60 sts).

Purl 1 round.

Cast off knitwise.

Spadix

With orange yarn and size 3.00mm needles, cast on 20 sts.

Row 1: k all sts tbl.

Row 2: k16, turn.

Row 3: sl 1, k to end.

Row 4: k12, turn.

Row 5: sl 1, k to end.

Row 6: k to end.

Knit 6 rows.

Cast off.

Stem

With green yarn and two double-pointed needles, cast on 5 sts.

Row 1: k5; do not turn but slide sts to other end of needle.

Rep this row until work measures 6.5cm (2½in); fasten off.

Making up

Stitch the cast-on and cast-off edges of the spadix together to form a tube. Stitch the base to the top of the stem. Insert into the flower and secure at the flower base.

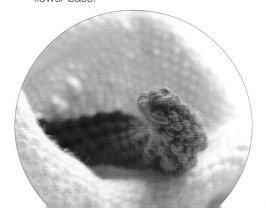

Materials:

Double knitting cotton yarn, white

Pure wool double knitting yarn, orange

Pure wool double knitting yarn, green

Needles:

Set of 5 double-pointed knitting needles, 3.00mm (UK 11; US 2)

1 pair 3.00mm (UK 11; US 2) knitting needles

Measurements:

Finished flower measures 18cm (7⅛in) long, including stem

To create an alternative lily, use a pure wool double knitting yarn in deep pink-violet for the main part of the flower.

Daisy

Instructions:

Petals (made in one piece)

With white cotton yarn and size 2.25mm (UK 13; US 1) needles, cast on 14 sts.

Row 1: k all sts tbl.

Row 2: k11, turn.

Row 3: k to end.

Row 4: k.

Row 5: cast off 12, k rem st.

Row 6: k2, cast on 12.

Rep rows 1–6 14 times, omitting row 6 on final rep and casting off last 2 sts instead.

Break yarn and fasten off.

Centre

With yellow bouclé yarn and size 2.25mm needles, cast on 6 sts.

Row 1: k.

Row 2: inc 1, k to last st, inc 1 (8 sts).

Row 3: k.

Row 4: inc 1, k to last st, inc 1 (10 sts).

Row 5: k.

Row 6: inc 1, k to last st, inc 1 (12 sts).

Knit 8 rows.

Row 15: sl 1, k1, psso, k8, k2tog (10 sts).

Row 16: k.

Row 17: sl 1, k1, psso, k6, k2tog (8 sts).

Row 18: k.

Row 19: sl 1, k1, psso, k4, k2tog (6 sts).

Cast off.

Making up

Join the two ends of the petals to form a ring. Stitch a gathering thread along the base of all the petals and pull up tightly to gather.

Stitch a running thread around the edge of the centre piece, place the button inside and pull up the yarn to gather; fasten off securely.

Stitch the covered button to the centre of the flower.

Materials:

Cotton double knitting yarn, white

Acrylic double knitting bouclé yarn, yellow

Round button, 3cm (1¼in)

Needles:

1 pair 2.25mm (UK 13; US 1) knitting needles

Tapestry needle

Measurements:

Finished flower measures 15cm (6in) across

Use the white daisy to decorate a summer hat or beach bag. Use blue yarn to make a Michaelmas daisy, or create a customised daisy in your favourite colour.

Rose

Instructions:

Petal (make 6)

With red yarn and size 3.00mm (UK 11; US 2)
needles, cast on 2 sts.

Row 1: inc in each st (4 sts).

Row 2: inc 1, k to end.

Row 3: inc 1, p to last st, k1.

Rep rows 2 and 3 until there are 10 sts.

Knit 8 rows.

Next row: k2tog, k6, k2tog (8 sts).

Next row: k2tog, p4, k2tog.

Next row: k2tog, k2, K2tog.

Next row: k2tog twice.

Next row: k2tog.

Fasten off.

Flower centre

With red yarn and size 3.00mm needles, cast on 108 sts.

Row 1: k all sts tbl.

Row 2: p2tog to end of row (54 sts).

Row 3: k.

Row 4: (p2tog, p4) to end of row (45 sts).

Row 5: k.

Row 6: (p2tog, p3) to end of row (36 sts).

Row 7: k.

Row 8: p2tog to end of row (18 sts).

Row 9: k.

Row 10: p2tog to end of row (9 sts).
Break yarn and thread through rem sts.

Making up

Curl the centre into a spiral and pull up the tail of yarn to gather the base, then secure it with a few stitches.

Stitch petals one at a time around the centre, with the cast-off edge of each petal at the base of the flower.

Opposite

A rose makes the perfect corsage on a coat, jacket or sweater. A cluster of roses would make a pretty decoration for a hat or bag. Pink yarn also makes a lovely rose – but roses come in all colours, so choose your favourite.

Materials:

Pure wool double knitting yarn, red

Needles:

Pair of knitting needles, 3.00mm (UK 11; US 2)

Tapestry needle

Measurements:

Finished flower measures 8cm (3¹/₈in) across

Snowdrop

Instructions:

Stem

With a set of four 2.75mm (UK 12; US 2) double-pointed needles and yarn A, cast on 9 sts and divide between three of the needles, using the fourth to knit with.

Rounds 1–4: knit.

Round 5: (sl 1, k1, psso, k1) 3 times (6 sts).

Round 6: (sl 1, k1, psso) 3 times (3 sts).

Round 7: k1, k2tog, do not turn but slide sts to the other end of needle.

Row 8: k2; do not turn but slide sts to other end of needle. Rep this row 42 times.

Cast off.

Petals

With 2.75mm (UK 12; US 2) needles and B, cast on 6 sts.

Row 1: purl.

Row 2: knit.

Row 3: purl.

Row 4: k2, turn and leave unworked sts on a spare needle.

Row 5: purl.

Row 6: knit.

Row 7: purl.

Row 8: (inc1) twice (4 sts).

Row 9: purl.

Row 10: k1, (inc1) twice, k1 (6 sts).

Beg with a purl row, work 7 rows in stocking stitch.

Row 18: k1, sl 1, k1, psso, k2tog, k1 (4 sts).

Row 19: purl.

Row 20: k1, sl1, k1, psso, k1 (3 sts).

Row 21: p3tog; cut yarn and fasten off. Rejoin yarn to sts on spare needle and rep rows 4–21 twice more.

Opposite

Snowdrops are the first sign of spring in many countries, so add this hopeful sign to your winter clothes!

Materials:

4-ply (fingering) wool yarn in dark green (A) and ecru (B)

Needles:

Pair of knitting needles, 2.75mm (UK 12; US 2)

Set of four double-pointed knitting needles, 2.75mm (UK 12; US 2)

Tapestry needle

Measurements:

Finished flower 17cm (6¾in) long, including stem

Making up

Join the ends of the cast-on edges of the petals and stitch the first few rows together to form a tight tube, then insert this into the 'cup' at the top of the stem. Stitch the edge of the cup round the narrow parts of the petals using tail of yarn A. Weave in all remaining yarn ends.

Viola

Instructions:

Large petals (make 2)
With 2.75mm (UK 12; US 2) needles and yarn A, cast on 7 sts.

Row 1: (inc 1 in first stitch) k5, inc 1 in last stitch (9 sts).

Row 2: purl.

Row 3: (inc 1 in first stitch) k7, inc 1 in last stitch (11 sts).

Row 4: purl.

Row 5: knit.

Row 6: purl.

Row 7: k2tog tbl, k7, k2tog (9 sts).

Row 8: purl.

Row 9: k2tog tbl, k5, k2tog (7 sts).

Row 10: purl.

Row 11: k2tog tbl, sl1, k2tog, psso, k2tog (3 sts).

Row 12: p3 tog; fasten off.

Small petals (make 3)
With same needles and B, cast on 5 sts.

Row 1: (inc 1 in first stitch) k3, inc 1 in last stitch (7 sts).

Row 2: purl.

Row 3: (inc 1 in first stitch) k5, inc 1 in last stitch (9 sts).

Row 4: purl.

Row 5: knit.

Row 6: purl.

Row 7: k2tog tbl, k5, k2tog (7 sts).

Row 8: purl.

Row 9: k2tog tbl, k3, k2tog (5 sts).

Row 10: purl.

Row 11: k2tog tbl, k1, k2tog (3 sts).

Row 12: p3tog; fasten off.

Making up
Join the cast-off points of the three small petals together at the centre. Place the two large petals behind and stitch all five together at the centre; petals will overlap slightly. Thread a tapestry needle with a short length of pale green yarn and embroider a few stitches to form the flower centre, then thread the needle with a short length of yarn B and embroider a few longer straight stitches, radiating out from centre, using the picture of the finished flower as a guide.

Materials:
4-ply (fingering) wool yarn in lavender (A), yellow (B) and green (B)

small amounts of 4-ply yarn in pale green and dark green

Needles:
Pair of knitting needles, 2.75mm (UK 12; US 2)

Tapestry needle

Opposite
Stitch the viola to a napkin ring, a hat band or a baby's bonnet. To make the purple alternative, knit all petals in yarn B. Embroider the centre using pale green and yellow yarn. To make a stem, take six strands of dark green and make a three-stranded plait (three groups of two strands) of the desired length. Knot the ends and trim, then stitch one end to the back of the flower.

Passionflower

Instructions:

Petals

*With 2.75mm (UK 12; US 2) needles and yarn A, cast on 2 sts.
Row 1: knit.

Row 2: (inc 1) twice (4 sts).

Row 3: sl 1, knit to end.

Rows 4–6: as row 3.

Row 7: k1, M1, knit to last st, M1, k1 (6 sts).

Rep rows 3–7 twice more (10 sts).

Row 23: sl 1, knit to end.

Rep row 23 nineteen times.

Row 43: k1, sl 1, k1, psso, k4, k2tog, k1 (8 sts).

Cut yarn and transfer stitches to a holder.**

Rep from * to ** four times more; do not cut yarn after completing fifth petal; keep these stitches on needle.

Join petals.

Row 1: k5, then knit across all sts on holder (40 sts); cut yarn A and join in yarn C.

Row 2: k7, (k2tog, k6) 4 times, k1 (36 sts).

Row 3: knit.

Row 4: (k4, k2tog) 6 times (30 sts).

Row 5: knit.

Row 6: (k3, k2tog) 6 times (24 sts).

Row 7: knit.

Row 8: (k2, k2tog) 6 times (18 sts).

Row 9: knit.

Row 10: (k1, k2tog) 6 times (12 sts)

Row 11: (k2tog) 6 times.

Cut yarn and thread tail through rem 6 sts.

Make a second set of petals in exactly the same way but using yarn B instead of A.

Stamens, outer (make 5)

With the double-pointed needles and yarn D, cast on 3 sts.
Row 1: k3; do not turn but slide sts to other end of needle. Rep this row 8 times.

Row 10: inc 1 in each stitch (6 sts).

Beg with a purl row, work 4 rows in stocking stitch.

Cast off purlwise.

Stamens, inner (make 3)

With 2.75mm (UK 12; US 2) needles and yarn D, cast on 20 sts.

Row 1: (inc 1 in each of first 10 sts), knit to end.

Cast off, knitting each st tbl.

Fringe

With 2.75mm (UK 12; US 2) needles and yarn E, cast on 36 sts.

Row 1: *knit next st but do not transfer to right-hand needle, yfwd between needles, loop yarn around thumb at front of work, yb between needles, knit into back of st, then pass 1st st over 2nd st; rep from * to end of row.

Row 2: knit.

Cast off, knitting each st tbl.

Materials:

4-ply (fingering) wool yarn in azure blue (A), violet (B), pale yellow (C), pale green (D) and lilac (E)

Needles:

Pair of knitting needles, 2.75mm (UK 12; US 2)

Two 2.75mm (UK 12; US 2) double-pointed needles

Stitch holder

Tapestry needle

Measurements:

Finished flower is 15cm (6in) in diameter

Making up

On each set of petals, bring the two edges of the knitting together to make a circle of petals and stitch the lower corners of the two end petals together; pull the yarn tail to close the hole in the centre. Place one on top of the other, making sure petals are offset, then stitch the centres firmly together. Stitch the cast-off edge of the fringe in place round the edge of the flower centre, then snip through each loop of yarn. Roll up the cast-off edge on top of each of the outer stamens, then stitch the base of each stamen in place. Curl the top of each of the inner stamens to form a cup shape, then stitch the base of each inner stamen in place in the centre of the flower. Weave in any remaining ends of yarn.

This beautiful passionflower makes a striking embellishment on a knitted cushion cover – if you can resist wearing it!

Pelargonium

Instructions:

Petal (make 5)

With 3.00mm (UK 11; US 2) needles and yarn A, cast on 9 sts.

Row 1: purl.

Row 2: k7, turn.

Row 3: p5, turn.

Row 4: k3, turn.

Row 5: p1, turn.

Row 6: knit to end.

Row 7: purl.

Row 8: k3, sl 1, k2tog, psso, k3 (7 sts).

Row 9: purl.

Row 10: k2, sl 1, k2tog, psso, k2 (5 sts).

Row 11: purl.

Row 12: k1, sl 1, k2tog, psso, k1 (3 sts).

Row 13: purl.

Row 14: sl 1, k2tog, psso; fasten off.

Making up

Stitch the narrow cast-off edges of the petals together. To make a stalk, cut three lengths of green yarn, each about 25cm (10in) long. Fold each strand in half and loop the folds around a fixed object (such as a drawing pin pushed in to a piece of wood). Plait the strands in pairs, then knot the cut ends together and trim.

Opposite

These bright red beauties bring the freshness of the garden indoors.

Materials:

4-ply (fingering) wool yarn in red (A) and green (B)

Needles:

Pair of knitting needles, 3.00mm (UK 11; US 2)

Tapestry needle

Measurements:

Finished flower 6.5cm (2½in) in diameter

Peony

Instructions:

Petals

*With 3.00mm (UK 11; US 2) needles and yarn A, cast on 5 sts. Row 1: knit.

Row 2: (inc 1 in each stitch) (10 sts).

Row 3: knit.

Row 4: (k1, inc 1 in next stitch) 5 times (15 sts).

Knit 10 rows.

Row 15: k13, turn.

Row 16: k11, turn.

Row 17: k9, turn.

Row 18: k7, turn.

Row 19: k5, turn.

Row 20: k3, turn.

Row 21: knit to end.

Knit 10 rows.

Row 32: (k1, k2tog) 5 times (10 sts).

Row 33: knit.

Row 34: (k2tog) 5 times (5 sts).

Cut yarn and transfer stitches to a holder.**

Rep from * to ** four times more; do not cut yarn after completing fifth petal; keep these stitches on needle.

Join petals.

Row 1: k5, then knit across all sts on holder (25 sts).

Row 2: k4, (k2tog, k3) 4 times, k4 (21 sts).

Row 3: knit.

Row 4: (k2tog) 10 times, k1.

Cast off.

Make a second set of petals in exactly the same way.

Stamens

With 3.00mm (UK 11; US 2) needles and yarn B, *cast on 14 sts, cast off 12 sts; transfer last stitch worked from right-hand to left-hand needle; rep from * 19 times more (40 sts).

Row 1: knit.

Cast off.

Making up

On each set of petals, bring the two edges of the knitting together to make a circle of petals and stitch the lower corners of the two end petals together; run a gathering stitch around the centre, along the base of each petal and pull up tightly to gather. Place one on top of the other, making sure petals are offset, then stitch centres firmly together. Roll up the cast-off edge of the row of stamens into a spiral, stitching the edges together to secure them as you go. Stitch the base of this spiral of stamens securely to the centre of the flower. Weave in any remaining ends of yarn.

Materials:

4-ply (fingering) wool yarn in deep pink (A)

4-ply (fingering) wool-silk blend yarn in yellow (B)

Needles:

Pair of knitting needles, 3.00mm (UK 11; US 2)

Stitch holder

Tapestry needle

Measurements:

Finished flower 14cm (5½in) in diameter

Opposite

As an alternative, mwake the petals in a white yarn: the petals on this one are knitted in a wool and silk blend, with the stamens in a pure wool yarn.

Lavender

Instructions:

Stem
With 2.75mm (UK 12; US 2) double-pointed needles and yarn A, cast on 3 sts.

Row 1: k3; do not turn but slide sts to other end of needle. Rep this row 65 times; cut yarn A and join in yarn B.

Calyx cluster
Row 1: (inc 1 in each stitch) (6 sts).

Row 2: purl.

Row 3: (k1, inc 1 in next stitch) (9 sts).

Row 4: purl.

Row 5: k1, (cast on 3 sts, cast off 3 sts), k1.

Row 6: purl.

Row 7: (sl1, k2tog, psso) 3 times (3 sts); do not turn but cut yarn B and rejoin yarn A.

Continued stem
With RS facing, k3; do not turn but slide sts to other end of needle Rep this row 7 times; cut yarn A and rejoin yarn B.

Flower head
Row 1: (inc 1 in each stitch) (6 sts).

Row 2: purl.

Row 3: (k1, inc 1 in next stitch) (9 sts).

Row 4: purl.

Row 5: (k1, cast on 3 sts, cast off 3 sts) 4 times, k1.

Row 6: purl.

Rep rows 5 and 6 once more.

Row 9: k1, (cast on 3 sts, cast off 3 sts) 7 times, k1.

Row 10: purl.

Rep rows 9 and 10 twice more.

Row 15: (k1, cast on 3 sts, cast off 3 sts) 4 times, k1.

Row 16: (p3 tog) 3 times.

Cut yarn and thread tail through rem 3 sts.

Making up
Use yarn tails to stitch the sides of the calyx cluster and the flower head. Weave in any remaining ends of yarn.

Materials:
4-ply (fingering) wool yarn in pale green (A) and lavender (B)

Needles:
Pair of knitting needles, 2.75mm (UK 12; US 2)

Two double-pointed knitting needles, 2.75mm (UK 12; US 2)

Tapestry needle

Measurements:
Finished flower 29cm (11½in) long, including stem

Lavender makes a gorgeous detail. You could make several stems and tie them with ribbon to create a finishing touch for clothes, bags or household accessories.

Crocus

Materials:

4-ply (fingering) wool yarn in violet (A), yellow (B) and emerald green (C)

Needles:

Pair of knitting needles, 2.75mm (UK 12; US 2)

Two double-pointed knitting needles, 2.75mm (UK 12; US 2)

Tapestry needle

Measurements:

Finished flower 14cm (5½in) long, including stem

Instructions:

Flower petal (make 6)

With 2.75mm (UK 12; US 2) needles and yarn A, cast on 2 sts.

Row 1 (WS): purl.

Row 2: k1, M1, k1 (3 sts).

Row 3: purl.

Row 4: k1, M1, k1, M1, k1 (5 sts).

Row 5: purl.

Row 6: k1, M1, k3, M1, k1 (7 sts).

Row 7: purl.

Row 8: k5, turn.

Row 9: p3, turn.

Row 10: knit to end.

Row 11: purl.

Row 12: knit.

Row 13: p5, turn.

Row 14: k3, turn.

Row 15: purl to end.

Row 16: knit.

Row 17: purl.

Row 18: k5, turn,

Row 19: p3, turn.

Row 20: knit to end.

Row 21: purl.

Row 22: sl1, k1, psso, k3, k2tog (5 sts).

Row 23: p2tog, p1, p2tog tbl (3 sts).

Row 24: sl1, k2tog, psso.

Cut yarn and thread tail through rem st.

Stamens (make 2)

With 2.75mm (UK 12; US 2) double-pointed needles and yarn B, cast on 2 sts. Row 1: k2; do not turn but slide sts to other end of needle. Rep this row 19 times.

Cast off.

Stalk and leaf

With 2.75mm (UK 12; US 2) double-pointed needles and yarn C, cast on 2 sts. Row 1: k2; do not turn but slide sts to other end of needle Rep this row 29 times.

Row 31: (inc 1 in each stitch) (4 sts).

Row 32: purl.

Row 33: k2, M1, k2 (5 sts).

Beg with a purl row, work 13 rows in stocking stitch.

Row 47: sl1, k1, psso, k1, k2tog (3 sts).

Beg with a purl row, work 19 rows in stocking stitch.

Row 67: sl 1, k2tog, psso.

Cut yarn and thread through rem st.

Making up

Fold the leaf upwards where it joins at the base of the i-cord stem. Wrap the widest part of leaf around the base of the stem and stitch the side edges of the leaf together. Fold each stamen in half and stitch the folds to the top of the i-cord stem. Stitch the cast-on edge of each petal to the top of the stem, enclosing the stamens. Weave in any remaining ends of yarn.

The crocus looks lovely around the home but would also liven up a winter coat, pinned to the lapel as a promise of spring.

Allium

Materials:

Tweedy aran-weight bouclé
yarn in violet and ecru mix (A)

4-ply (fingering) wool or wool
blend yarn in sage green (B)

Pipe cleaner, 30cm (11¾in)

Polyester toy filling

Needles:

Set of four double-pointed
knitting needles, 3.25mm
(UK 10, US 3)

Pair of knitting needles, 3.25mm
(UK 10, US 3)

Tapestry needle

Measurements:

Flower head 7cm (2¾in)
diameter, stalk 28cm (11in)

Instructions:

Flower head

With the double-pointed needles
and yarn A, cast on 6 sts and divide
equally between three needles,
using the fourth to knit with.

Round 1: (inc 1 in each stitch)
(12 sts).

Round 2: (k1, inc 1 in next stitch)
(18 sts).

Round 3: (k2, inc 1 in next stitch)
(24 sts).

Round 4: (k3, inc 1 in next stitch)
(30 sts).

Round 5: knit.

Round 6: (k4, inc 1 in next stitch)
(36 sts).

Knit 12 rounds.

Round 19: (k4, k2tog) 6 times
(30 sts).

Round 20: knit.

Round 21: (k3, k2tog) 6 times
(24 sts).

Round 22: (k2, k2tog) 6
times (18 sts).

Round 23: (k1, k2tog) 6
times (12 sts).

Round 24: (k2tog)
6 times.

Cut yarn and thread tail
through rem 6 sts.

Stalk

With two 3.25mm (UK
10, US 3) needles and
yarn B, cast on 75 sts.

Beg with a purl row,

work 5 rows in stocking stitch.

Cast off.

Making up

Stuff the flower head with polyester
filling; make sure it is firm but do
not overstuff as this will stretch
the knitted fabric and spoil the
appearance. Pull the yarn tail to
close the stitches at the top. To
make the stalk, wrap the strip of
knitting around a pipe cleaner and
stitch cast-on and cast-off edges
together. Insert one end of the stalk
into the base of the flower head
and use yarn tails to stitch the two
together. Weave in any remaining
ends of yarn.

Opposite

*To make the flower head extra
fluffy, use a wire brush or a teasel
to comb the surface of the knitted
fabric. For a smaller version, follow
the same pattern but for the head,
use a 4-ply mohair-blend yarn and
2.75mm (UK 12; US 2) needles.*

Crocheted Flowers

by Jan Ollis

Accessorising can complete an outfit, revitalise a well-loved hat, even add interest to decorations around the home. It is a cheap and relatively quick way of adding those little details that can be expensive to buy on the high street.

I have had great fun designing these twenty-eight crocheted flowers. Most of the patterns need only tiny amounts of materials, making them ideal for using up those half-used balls of yarn, scraps of pretty fabric, beads, buttons and ribbons we all have lying around at home and which 'will come in useful one day'. The yarn I use is mainly no. 3 crochet cotton, which is wonderfully easy to use, though some patterns use other weights of yarn as well as speciality yarns such as fluffy and ribbon yarn. New yarns are being developed all the time and it is exciting to try these out to get different effects.

I have used various crochet hook sizes to make the flowers, and these are given at the start of each project. It is great fun experimenting with different hook sizes and types of yarn; if the flowers turn out slightly different from mine, it doesn't matter at all – it is far better to enjoy the process of making them, and to create something that is unique and personal to you. For this reason, I've given no guidance on tension/gauge, as this will vary depending on the size of hook or type of yarn you use.

Have fun embellishing the flowers as well. Try adding a large, bright button to the centre of the Retro Daisy and stitch it on to a denim jacket or jeans. Make a smaller version of the Camellia, perhaps, and attach it to a hairslide, or make numerous Gazanias in all different colours and sew them on to a plain cushion. I've made all the patterns as easy as possible, so even if you are just learning how to crochet, there will be something here for you. Enjoy!

The flowers

Peony, page 70

Pink Cosmos, page 72

Gazania, page 74

Tudor Rose, page 76

Clematis, page 78

Hibiscus, page 80

Foxgloves, page 82

White Water Lily, page 84

Poppy, page 86

Freesia, page 88

Daisy Chain, page 90

African Violets, page 92

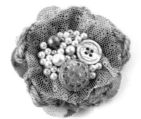

Camellia, page 94

Turquoise Passionflower,
page 96

Antique Rose, page 98

Retro Daisy, page 100

Carnation, page 40

Scabious, page 104

Black Orchid, page 106

Orange Blossom, page 108

Aquilegia, page 110

Sweet Peas, page 112

Red Anemone, page 114

Lisianthus, page 116

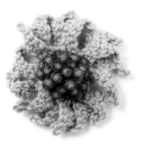

Echinacea, page 118

Auricula in pot, page 124

Lobelia, page 120

Narcissus, page 122

Peony

Instructions:

With dark red yarn and the larger hook, make 25 ch.

Row 1: miss 1 ch, 2 dc (*UK tr*) into each ch to end.

The work will curl naturally. Form it into 5 rolls, then sew together the ends, making sure the work all faces the same way. Sew together at the centre.

Flower centre

With light blue yarn and the smaller hook, make 5 ch, join with ss into a ring.

*2 ch, 1 dc (*UK tr*), 1 tr (*UK dtr*), 1 dc (*UK tr*), 2 ch, ss, all into centre of loop*, repeat from * to * 4 more times, making 5 petals in total.

Break off yarn, keeping a length of yarn for sewing the flower centre into the middle of the dark red flower.

Materials and equipment:

Bulky or super bulky yarn in dark red

Double knitting/sport weight yarn in light blue

Crochet hooks, sizes 4.50mm (US G, UK 7) and 2.50mm (US B-1, UK 13)

Bodkin or large-eyed needle for sewing the flower together

Add your own distinctive style to a plain hat with this stunning flower.

Pink Cosmos

Instructions:

With lime green crochet cotton, make a slip ring.

Round 1: 2 ch, sc (*UK dc*) into ring 8 times. Fasten off the lime green crochet cotton.

Change to pale green and ss together.

Round 2: 2 ch, hdc (*UK htr*) into each sc (*UK dc*) 8 times, 1 hdc (*UK htr*) into base ch of 2 ch, join in bright pink and ss into 2 ch.

Make the petal cluster:

*2 ch, 1 dc (*UK tr*), 1 tr (*UK dtr*), 1 dc (*UK tr*), 2 ch, ss, all into first ch of 2 ch, hdc (*UK htr*), sc (*UK dc*) into next hdc (*UK htr*)*, repeat from * to * 8 more times (making 9 petals in total).

Tie off and sew in the ends.

Materials and equipment:

No. 3 crochet cotton in lime green, pale green and bright pink

Crochet hook size 3.00mm (US D-0, UK 11)

Bodkin or large-eyed needle for sewing in the ends

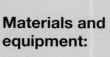

These lovely little flowers work in all sorts of colour combinations. Use them to decorate cushions, lampshades and throws around the home.

Gazania

Instructions:

Using colour A, make a slip ring.

Round 1: 1 ch, 10 sc (*UK dc*) into ring. Pull end to close ring.

Fasten off colour A and change to colour B.

ss into first sc (*UK dc*) of ring.

Round 2: 6 ch, ss into base ch, *sc (*UK dc*) into next sc (*UK dc*) of ring, 5 ch, ss into base sc (*UK dc*)*, repeat from * to * 9 times, making 10 petals in total.

Fasten off colour B and change to colour C.

Round 3: insert hook into base ch of first petal.

ss, 7 ch, *ss into base sc (*UK dc*) between petals 1 and 2, 6 ch*, repeat from * to * between each petal base, sc (*UK dc*) 9 times, ss into base of first petal.

Fasten off colour C and sew in the ends.

Materials and equipment:

No. 3 crochet cotton in 3 different colours (A, B and C from the centre outwards)

Crochet hook size 2.50mm (US B-1, UK 13)

Bodkin or large-eyed needle for sewing in the ends

Add a splash of colour to an otherwise plain pair of slippers with these fanciful flowers.

Tudor Rose

Instructions:

For the flower centre, use white crochet cotton and make 4 ch, join with ss into a ring.

*3 ch, 3 tr (*UK dtr*), 3 ch, ss into ring*, repeat from * to * 4 more times, making 5 petals in total. Fasten off.

Using red for the back of the flower, make 6 ch, join with ss into a ring.

*4 ch, 5 dtr (*UK ttr*), 4 ch, ss into ring*, repeat from * to * 4 more times, making 5 petals in total. Fasten off.

Using green for the leaves, make 8 ch, join with ss into a ring.

*7 ch, miss 1 ch, sc (*UK dc*) into next ch, 2 dc (*UK tr*), 3 tr (*UK dtr*),

ss into ring*, repeat from * to * 3 more times.

7 ch, miss 1 ch, ss into next ch, sc (*UK dc*) into next ch, 2 dc (*UK tr*), 2 dtr (*UK ttr*), ss into base of first leaf. Fasten off.

Lay the red flower on the leaves so that the leaves are visible between each petal. Sew together.

Lay the white flower on the red flower so that the red petals lie between the white petals. Sew together invisibly.

Sew the large pearl-shaped bead into the centre of the white flower, and sew the smaller yellow beads around it.

Materials and equipment:

No. 3 crochet cotton in white, red and lime green

Crochet hook size 3.00mm (US D-0, UK 11)

Selection of small yellow beads

1 large pearl-shaped bead (pale yellow)

Sewing needle and thread

Bodkin or large-eyed needle for sewing the flower together

This gorgeous flower is easy to crochet and will add a unique touch to your home.

Clematis

Instructions:

Turquoise flower

With turquoise crochet cotton, make 6 ch, ss into loop.

10 ch, ss into loop, repeat from * to * 4 more times, making 5 petals in total.

*ss in first 10 ch loop, 2 sc (*UK dc*), 2 hdc (*UK htr*), 2 dc (*UK tr*), 1 hdc (*UK htr*), 2 sc (*UK dc*), 1 ss, 2 sc (*UK dc*), 1 hdc (*UK htr*), 2 dc (*UK tr*), 2 hdc (*UK htr*), 2 sc (*UK dc*), ss into loop*, repeat from * to * into each 6 ch loop.
Fasten off.

Pink flower

Work as for turquoise flower using bright pink crochet cotton. Then:

*ss pale pink into first st on outside of a petal, sc (*UK dc*) into each ch st formed 10 times, 1 ch, ss into same base ch, 10 sc (*UK dc*) down left-hand side of petal, ss into ring*, repeat from * to * around each petal.

Tie off and cut the ends.

Opposite

What better way to personalise a favourite item than to add a handmade flower in a coordinating colour?

Materials and equipment:

No. 3 crochet cotton in turquoise, pale pink and bright pink

Crochet hook size 3.00mm (US D-0, UK 11)

Bodkin or large-eyed needle for sewing in the ends

Hibiscus

Instructions:

With purple crochet cotton, make 8 ch, sc (*UK dc*) into 3rd ch, sc (*UK dc*) to end, turn [6 sts].

Row 1: 1 ch, miss 1 ch, sc (*UK dc*) into next 6 ch, turn.

Row 2: 1 ch, sc (*UK dc*) into next 5 sc (*UK dc*), 2 sc (*UK dc*) into last sc (*UK dc*), turn.

Row 3: 1 ch, sc (*UK dc*) into next 6 sc (*UK dc*), 2 sc (*UK dc*) into last sc (*UK dc*), turn.

Row 4: 1 ch, sc (*UK dc*) into next 7 sc (*UK dc*), 2 sc (*UK dc*) into last sc (*UK dc*), turn.

Row 5: 1 ch, sc (*UK dc*) into next 8 sc (*UK dc*), 2 sc (*UK dc*) into last sc (*UK dc*), turn.

Row 6: 1 ch, sc (*UK dc*) into next 9 sc (*UK dc*), 2 sc (*UK dc*) into last sc (*UK dc*), turn.

Row 7: 1 ch, sc (*UK dc*) into next 10 sc (*UK dc*), 2 sc (*UK dc*) into last sc (*UK dc*), turn.

Row 8: 1 ch, miss 1 sc (*UK dc*), sc (*UK dc*) into next 11 sc (*UK dc*), turn.

Rows 9 and 10: repeat row 8 twice.

Row 11: 1 ch, miss 2 sc (*UK dc*), 7 sc (*UK dc*), miss 2 sc (*UK dc*), ss into last sc (*UK dc*).

Row 12: ss, 1 sc (*UK dc*), 2 hdc (*UK htr*) into same sc (*UK dc*), 1 ch, ss into next sc (*UK dc*), ss into next sc (*UK dc*), 1 ch, 2 hdc (*UK htr*) into next sc (*UK dc*), 1 sc (*UK dc*) into next sc (*UK dc*), ss into next sc (*UK dc*).

Fasten off.

Repeat all the above instructions, making 5 petals in total.

For the flower centre, thread the orange beads on to the orange crochet cotton, finishing with the white bead. Make a knot at one end.

Push the white bead up to the knot and ch st around it. Make 1 ch then ch st around an orange bead. Continue to ch st around the beads in the order in which they are threaded. If the flower centre is too loose, wrap the remaining crochet cotton around the beads to make it stable.

Layer the petals so that they overlap slightly leaving a 1cm (½in) hole in the centre. Sew gathering stitches along the bottom edges of all the petals. Draw them together slightly. Place the wider end of the orange-beaded flower centre through this hole and sew it in place securely.

Materials and equipment:

No. 3 crochet cotton in purple and orange

Crochet hook size 3.00mm (US D-0, UK 11)

1 small white bead

15 larger orange beads

Sewing needle and thread

Bodkin or large-eyed needle for sewing the flower together

Opposite

This exotic flower works well in bright, tropical colours. Use it to brighten up your summer clothes, bags and accessories.

Foxgloves

Instructions:

With pale pink crochet cotton, make a slip ring. 2 ch, 9 sc (*UK dc*), pull together, join with a ss.

Round 1: 2 ch, sc (*UK dc*) into next 9 sc (UK dc), join with ss into 2 ch sp.

Round 2: repeat round 1.

Round 3: 2 ch, 9 hdc (*UK htr*), ss into 2 ch.

Round 4: 3 ch, 9 dc (*UK tr*), ss into 2 ch.

Round 5: 3 ch, 9 dc (*UK tr*), 1 sc (*UK dc*), turn.

Round 6: miss 1 ch, sc (*UK dc*), 2 hdc (*UK htr*) into same dc (*UK tr*), 1 dc (*UK tr*), 1 tr (*UK dtr*), 3 dtr (*UK ttr*) into same dc (*UK tr*), 1 tr (*UK dtr*), 1 dc (*UK tr*), 2 hdc (*UK htr*) into same dc (*UK tr*), 1 sc (*UK dc*), 1 ss.

Tie off and sew in the ends.

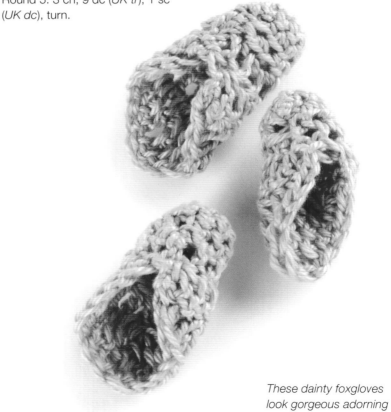

Materials and equipment:

No. 3 crochet cotton in pale pink

Crochet hook size 2.50mm (US B-1, UK 13)

Bodkin or large-eyed needle for sewing in the ends

These dainty foxgloves look gorgeous adorning tablecloths or napkins.

White Water Lily

Instructions:

Take a long length of sewing cotton, fold it in half and thread the cut ends through the eye of the sewing needle, forming a large loop. Thread the crochet cotton into the bodkin needle and push the bodkin needle and crochet cotton through the cotton loop. Thread the beads on to the sewing needle, push them on to the sewing thread and the crochet thread. Thread on 42 beads for the centre petals and 72 for the outer petals.

Centre petals (make 6)

Make 7 ch using ivory crochet cotton.

Materials and equipment:

No. 3 crochet cotton in ivory, yellow and green

Crochet hook size 3.00mm (US D-0, UK 11)

Small crystal beads

Sewing needle and cotton thread

Bodkin or large-eyed needle for sewing the flower together

Miss 2 ch, ss, 1 ch, sc (UK dc) into next 5 sc (UK dc), ss across base, sc (UK dc) into next 5 ch from other side of ch, ss into top ch, 1 ch, ss into next sc (UK dc), sc (UK dc) into next 5 sc (UK dc) to base.

Turn and begin to insert beads. ss into base ch, *ss with bead into next ch, ss without bead into next ch*, repeat from * to * twice more, ss with bead into next ch, ss into top ch, 2 ch, miss 1 ch, ss with bead, *ss with bead into next ch, ss without bead into next ch*, repeat from * to * 3 more times.

Tie off the end, leave a long length for sewing in. This makes 1 petal.

Outer petals (make 8)

Make 9 ch with ivory crochet cotton.

Miss 2 ch, ss, 1 ch, sc (UK dc) into next 7 sc (UK dc), ss across base, sc (UK dc) into next 6 ch from other side of ch, ss into top ch, 1 ch, ss into base sc (UK dc), sc (UK dc) into next 7 sc (UK dc) to base.

Turn and begin to insert beads. *ss into next ch, ss with bead into next ch*, repeat from * to * 3 more times, ss with beads into top ch, 3 ch, miss 2 ch, ss with bead, *ss with bead into next ch, ss into next ch*, repeat from * to * 3 more times, ss with bead.

Tie off the end, leave a long length for sewing in. This makes 1 petal.

Stamen

Wrap yellow crochet cotton around a piece of card, 5 ch wide, 6 times. Slide the yarn off the card. Wrap

one end of the loops securely and leave a long length of thread for sewing. Pass these loops through the hole in the centre of the flower to the back, secure them, then cut through the loops on the front of the flower to make strands.

Leaves

With green crochet cotton, make a slip ring, 2 ch, 6 sc (UK dc), pull to join, ss into 2 ch.

Round 1: 2 ch, then 2 dc (UK tr) into each sc (UK dc) 6 times, turn.

Round 2: 2 ch, then dc (UK tr) into each dc (UK tr), 2 ch into 2 ch sp, turn.

Round 3: sc (UK dc) into next dc (UK tr), *2 dc (UK tr) into next dc (UK tr) three times, 3 dc (UK tr) into next dc (UK tr)*, repeat from * to * 5 times, 1 sc (UK dc) into next dc (UK tr) twice, 1 sc (UK dc) into 2 ch sp, ss into next ch, fasten off.

To make up

Thread the length of yarn attached to one of the centre petals through the bodkin needle, take it across the base of the petal and down on the other side. Pull the yarn so that the petal curls gently inwards. Tie off and cut the thread. Repeat this with the remaining five centre petals and the eight outer petals.

Take a length of ivory crochet cotton and sew the centre petals together to form a circle, with all the petals facing inwards. Sew the outer petals evenly around the centre petals. Tie off the end securely.

Poppy

Instructions:

With yellow yarn and a 3.50mm (US E-00, UK 9) crochet hook, *make 5 ch.

Row 1: miss 2 ch, 3 sc (UK dc), turn.

Row 2: 2 ch, dc (UK tr) into base sc (UK dc), dc (UK tr) into next 2 sc (UK dc), dc (UK tr) into last ch twice, turn.

Row 3: 2 ch, dc (UK tr) into base sc (UK dc), dc (UK tr) into next 3 dc (UK tr), 2 dc (UK tr) into last dc (UK tr), turn.

Row 4: 2 ch, dc (UK tr) into base dc (UK tr), dc (UK tr) into next 4 dc (UK tr), 2 dc (UK tr) into last dc (UK tr) sp, turn.

Row 5: miss 1 ch, ss, sc (UK dc), 3 hdc (UK htr), sc (UK dc), ss, turn.

Row 6: miss 1 ch, ss, 3 sc (UK dc), miss 1 ch, ss.

ss 6 sts down top side of petal.*

Do not cut yarn. Repeat from * to *, making 4 more petals.

Cut yarn, leave a long length of yarn for sewing in.

Use the tail of yarn to sew gathering stitches through each of the petals in sequence. Pull them together loosely and join petal 5 to petal 1. Tie and fasten off the yarn.

Tease the top of the petals to curl inwards.

Crochet button

With pale blue yarn and the 3.00mm (US D-0, UK 11) crochet hook, make a slip ring.

Row 1: 1 ch, 10 sc (UK dc) into ring, ss.

Row 2: 1 dc (UK tr) into next sc (UK dc), *2 dc (UK tr) into next sc (UK dc)*, repeat from * to * to end, ss into a ring.

Row 3: *1 dc (UK tr) into next sc (UK dc), miss next sc (UK dc)*, repeat from * to * to end, ss into a ring.

Cut and tie end of yarn, leaving a long length for sewing in.

Stuff with a small amount of toy stuffing.

Sew gathering stitches through the third round, draw up the yarn, sew in the end and fasten off.

Fabric

Fold in each short end of the fabric and press. Fold the fabric lengthways with wrong sides facing. Using sewing thread, sew gathering stitches along the open edge. Pull on the thread and draw the fabric into a circle, leaving a hole in the centre for the crochet button. Sew the sides together securely.

Place the fabric circle in the centre of the crocheted flower and sew them together securely. Stitch the crochet button in the centre of the fabric flower.

Materials and equipment:

Aran/worsted weight yarn in yellow

Double knitting/sport weight yarn in pale blue

Crochet hooks, sizes 3.00mm (US D-0, UK 11) and 3.50mm (US E-00, UK 9)

Toy stuffing

Patterned fabric, 22 x 5cm (8¾ x 2in)

Sewing needle and thread

Bodkin or large-eyed needle for sewing the flower together

Vary the colours and fabric used and create a stunning flower to match your own personal style.

Freesia

Instructions:

Using green crochet cotton, make a slip ring.

Round 1: 2 ch, sc (*UK dc*) 4 times, join with a ss into 2 ch.

Round 2: 2 ch, hdc (*UK htr*) 5 times into top stitch of sc (*UK dc*), ss into 2 ch.

Round 3: repeat round 2. Change to yellow when ss into 2 ch.

Round 4: 2 ch, *2 hdc (*UK htr*) into next ch,1 hdc (*UK htr*) into next ch*, repeat from * to * twice more, 1 hdc (*UK htr*), ss into 2 ch.

Petal cluster

In the yellow cotton, *3 ch, tr (*UK dtr*), dtr (*UK ttr*), tr (*UK dtr*), 3 ch, ss into base hdc (*UK htr*), ss into next hdc (*UK htr*), ss into next hdc (*UK htr*)*, repeat from * to * 3 more times to make 4 petals.

Tie off and sew in the ends.

Materials and equipment:

No. 3 crochet cotton in yellow and green

Crochet hook size 3.00mm (US D-0, UK 11)

Bodkin or large-eyed needle for sewing in the ends

Add a touch of springtime to your table with these pretty little freesias.

Daisy Chain

Instructions:

Single daisy

With yellow crochet cotton, make a slip ring.

Round 1: 1 ch, 8 sc (*UK dc*) into ring, pull end to close ring and remove hook.

Re-insert hook from back of work into first sc (*UK dc*) loop with a ss.

Round 2: change to white crochet cotton, *3 ch, ss into back of each of these 3 ch, ss into next base sc (*UK dc*)*, repeat from * to * 7 times, making 8 petals all together.

ss to centre and tie off the ends.

Double daisy

Follow the instructions for the single daisy up to the end of round 2.

Round 3: work into base ss between petals 1 and 2 of round 2, *sc (*UK dc*), 3 ch, ss into back of each of 3 ch to base ch*, repeat from * to * 7 more times.

sc (*UK dc*) to centre and tie off the ends.

Make seven daisies (some single and some double). Thread the green ribbon through the looped silver necklace and tie it in a knot at the back. Stitch daisies on to the ribbon at regular intervals.

Materials and equipment:

No. 3 crochet cotton in yellow and white

Crochet hook size 2.50mm (US B-1, UK 13)

70cm (27½in) silver-plated cable jewellery chain

100cm (39½in) green sheer organza ribbon

Sewing needle and thread

Who could resist this pretty necklace made with hand-crocheted daisies? Alternatively, make them into a stunning hairband or bracelet.

African Violets

Instructions:

With violet crochet cotton, make 4 ch, ss into a circle.

*1 ch, dc (*UK tr*), tr (*UK dtr*), dc (*UK tr*), 1 ch, ss, all into loop*, repeat from * to * 4 more times to make 5 petals.

Tie off the end and press the flower.

Change to yellow crochet cotton and make the central stamen.

3 ch, miss 2 ch, sc (*UK dc*) into ch, ss into base chain.

Tie off the end.

Insert the yellow stamen into the centre of the flower and sew it in place with sewing thread.

Leaf

With green crochet cotton, make a slip ring, 2 ch, 6 sc (*UK dc*), pull to join, ss into 2 ch.

Round 1: 2 ch, then 2 dc (*UK tr*) into each sc (*UK dc*) 6 times, turn.

Round 2: 2 sc (*UK dc*) into each dc (*UK tr*) 12 times, 1 sc (*UK dc*) into 2 ch, 2 dc (*UK tr*) into 2 ch, 1 sc (*UK dc*) into 2 ch, ss into 2 ch.

Fasten off.

Materials and equipment:

No. 3 crochet cotton in violet, yellow and green

Crochet hook size 2.50mm (US B-1, UK 13)

Sewing needle and thread

Bodkin or large-eyed needle for sewing in the ends

Bring a forgotten yet much-loved possession back to life with these brightly coloured flowers.

Camellia

Instructions:

Make 5 ch, join with ss into a ring.

*2 ch, 1 dc (*UK tr*), 1 tr (*UK dtr*),
1 dc (*UK tr*),
2 ch, ss, all into the centre of the loop*, repeat from * to * 4 more times to make 5 petals.

Break off the yarn.

Press the crocheted flower gently.

Cut a circle of lightweight fabric the same diameter as your flower.

Draw around the flower on tracing paper and cut out a template. Pin the template on to heavyweight fabric and cut out a fabric flower. Set aside.

Attach the lightweight fabric circle to the crocheted flower, stitching in a circle 1cm (½in) from the centre of the flower.

Sew buttons and large beads in the centre of the flower, then fill in the gaps with smaller beads.

Lay the beaded crocheted flower on to the heavyweight fabric flower and sew it in place invisibly from the back.

Materials and equipment:

Bulky or super bulky yarn in pink

Crochet hook size 4.50mm
(US G, UK 7)

Lightweight fabric, such as lace or voile

Heavyweight fabric, such as a furnishing cotton linen

Tracing paper

Pencil

Scissors

Assorted beads and vintage buttons

Sewing needle and thread

This design has a classic vintage feel. It works well in different colour combinations and with a variety of buttons and beads.

Turquoise Passionflower

Instructions:

Petals

Work from the centre of the flower outwards.

Using cream crochet cotton, make a slip ring.

2 ch, 6 sc (*UK dc*) into ring, pull to close, ss into top ch of 2 ch.

Round 1: 1 ch, 1 sc (*UK dc*) into base sc (*UK dc*), 2 sc (*UK dc*) into each of next 7 ch, ss into 1 ch.

Round 2: 1 ch,1 sc (*UK dc*), *2 sc (*UK dc*), 1 sc (*UK dc*), 1 sc (*UK dc*)*, repeat from * to * 4 more times, 1 sc (*UK dc*), ss into 1 ch.

Round 3: 1 ch, *2 sc (*UK dc*) into next sc (*UK dc*), 1 sc (*UK dc*) into next sc (*UK dc*)*, repeat from * to * 9 more times.

Join in the pale green crochet cotton and ss into 1 ch. Fasten off the cream cotton.

Using the pale green cotton, *10 ch, miss 2 ch, dc (*UK tr*) into next 4 ch, hdc (*UK htr*) into next 4 ch, ss into next sc (*UK dc*) of round 4, turn, ss into next 8 ch, sc (*UK dc*) into 2 ch sp, turn, dc (*UK tr*) into next 4 ch, hdc (*UK htr*) into next 4 ch, ss into next sc (*UK dc*) from round 3, ss into next sc (*UK dc*)*, repeat from * to * 9 more times. Fasten off.

Join the fluffy yarn at the base of petal 1, *3 ch, ss into base of next petal*, repeat from * to * 9 more times. Fasten off.

Flower centre

With lime green yarn, 4 ch, ss into ring, sc (*UK dc*) into ring, 4 ch, miss 1 ch, hdc (*UK htr*) into next ch, ss into next ch twice, ss into ring, *3 ch, miss 1 ch, hdc (*UK htr*) into next ch, ss into next ch, ss into ring*, repeat from * to * 3 more times. Fasten off.

With purple yarn, 3 ch, miss 1 ch, 1 hdc (*UK htr*), 1 ss. Place this in the middle of the lime green flower centre and sew it in place securely.

Sew the flower centre to the middle of the passion flower.

This stunning creation looks fabulous on clothes, bags and accessories.

Materials and equipment:

No. 3 crochet cotton in cream and pale green

Fluffy yarn in blue/black

Double knitting/sport weight yarn in lime green and purple

Crochet hook size 3.00mm (US D-0, UK 11)

Sewing needle and thread

Bodkin or large-eyed needle for sewing the flower together

Antique Rose

Instructions:

With blue yarn, make 100 ch.

1st Bud: miss 2 ch, 1 hdc (*UK htr*) into next ch, 1 dc (*UK tr*) into next ch, 1 hdc (*UK htr*) and 2 ch into next ch.

Petals 1–3: *ss into ch, 2 ch and 1 dc (*UK tr*) into next ch, 1 tr (*UK dtr*) into next ch, 1 dc (*UK tr*) and 2 ch into next ch*, repeat from * to * twice more.

Petals 4–6: *ss into ch, 2 ch and 1 dc (*UK tr*) into next ch, 1 dc (*UK tr*), 1 tr (*UK dtr*), 1 dc (*UK tr*) into next ch, 1 dc (*UK tr*) and 2 ch into next ch*, repeat from * to * twice more.

Petals 7–9: *ss into ch, 3 ch and 1 tr (*UK dtr*) into next ch, 1 tr (*UK dtr*), 1 dtr (*UK ttr*), 1 tr (*UK dtr*) into next ch, 1 tr (*UK dtr*) and 3 ch into next ch*, repeat from * to * twice more.

Petals 10–13: *ss into ch, 3 ch and 1 tr (*UK dtr*) into next ch, 2 tr (*UK dtr*), 1 dtr (*UK ttr*), 2 tr (*UK dtr*) into next ch, 1 tr (*UK dtr*) and 3 ch into next ch*, repeat from * to * 3 more times.

Petal 14: *ss into ch, 3 ch and 1 tr (*UK dtr*) into same ch, 1 tr (*UK dtr*) into next ch, 2 tr (*UK dtr*) into next ch, 2 dtr (*UK ttr*) into next ch (twice), 2 tr (*UK dtr*) into next ch, 1 tr (*UK dtr*) into next ch, 1 tr (*UK dtr*) and 3 ch into next ch*, repeat from * to * 3 more times.

Tie and cut the yarn.

Press the crocheted work and the length of fabric. Fray the edges of the fabric and lay it on top of the crochet, right side up. Sew gathering stitches along the bottom edge starting from the narrow end and working into the middle. Draw up the thread loosely, forming the shape of the flower. Secure the first half of the flower with a few stitches and repeat the process starting from the centre and working to the other end. Tie off the ends.

Materials and equipment:

Double knitting/sport weight yarn in blue

Crochet hook size 3.00mm (US D-0, UK 11)

Lightweight woven fabric, 60cm (23½in) long, tapering from 3 to 1cm (1¼ to ½in) evenly along one long edge

Sewing needle and thread

Bodkin or large-eyed needle for sewing the flower together

This pretty flower has a fresh, country feel. For a more vintage look, use peach-coloured crochet cotton and muted brown lace.

Retro Daisy

Instructions:

Orange flower

With orange crochet cotton, 8 ch, ss into ring.

Round 1: 1 ch, 12 sc (UK dc), join with ss.

Round 2: 9 ch, ss into base sc (UK dc), ss into next ch, ss into next ch, *10 ch, ss into next ch, ss into next ch*, repeat from * to * three more times, 10 ch, ss to next ch (makes 6 petals).

Round 3: *ss into centre of first 10 ch, 20 sc (UK dc) along length of ch, ss into base sc (UK dc)*, repeat from * to * 5 more times working into the centre of each 10 ch sp.

Cut and tie off the end.

Orange flower centre

Round 1: with purple crochet cotton, make a slip ring, 1 ch, 6 sc (UK dc).

Change to white crochet cotton, ss into 1 ch.

Round 2: 1 ch, 2 hdc (UK htr) in each sc (UK dc), ss into 1 ch.

Cut and tie off the ends.

Stalk

With dark green crochet cotton, make 20 ch, miss 1 ch, sc (UK dc) down length of ch, 1 ss across bottom of ch, 20 sc (UK dc) to top of ch.

Fasten off and sew in the ends.

Lay the flower centre in the middle of the orange daisy petals, sew them together securely and fasten off.

Turn the flower over, place the stalk so that the top is in the centre of the daisy petals and sew it in place securely with cotton thread.

Turquoise flower

This is made in the same way as the orange flower, but without the flower centre and stalk.

Yellow flower

With yellow crochet cotton, 6 ch, ss into ring.

Round 1: 1 ch, 10 sc (UK dc), join with ss.

Round 2: 7 ch, ss into base sc (UK dc), ss into next ch, ss into next ch, *8 ch, ss into next ch, ss into next ch*, repeat from * to * twice more, 8 ch, ss to next ch (makes 6 petals).

Round 3: *ss into centre of first 8 ch, 16 sc (UK dc) along length of ch, ss into base sc (UK dc)*, repeat from * to * 5 more times working into the centre of each 8 ch sp.

Cut and tie off the end.

Materials and equipment:

No. 3 crochet cotton in orange, purple, white, turquoise, yellow and dark green

Crochet hook size 3.00mm (US D-0, UK 11)

Sewing needle and thread

Bodkin or large-eyed needle for sewing in the ends

Add a splash of colour to your summer picnic or barbeque with these fun flowers.

Carnation

Instructions:

With red crochet cotton, make 31 ch.

Row 1: miss 1 ch, 2 dc (*UK tr*) into each ch, 1 ch, turn.

Row 2: 2 hdc (*UK htr*) into each ch, 1 ch, turn. Fasten off the red yarn and join in the pink.

Row 3: *3 ch into next ch, ss into next ch*, repeat from * to * to end of row.

Tie off the end, but leave a good length. Draw this length through the base chain in a loose gathering stitch. Pull up the work, tease the flowers into shape and pull the yarn through the petals to secure.

Small flower

To make a smaller flower you will need no. 1 crochet cotton in red and a size 2.50mm (US B-1, UK 13) crochet hook. Here I have made a pretty ring by attaching the flower to a ring base using fabric glue.

Make 25 ch.

Row 1: miss 2 ch, 2 sc (*UK dc*) into each ch to end, turn.

Row 2: miss ch, 2 sc (*UK dc*) into each sc (*UK dc*) from row 1.

Row 3: miss ch, 2 hdc (*UK htr*) into each sc (*UK dc*) from row 2 to last 10 sc (*UK dc*), 1 sc (*UK dc*) to end, 1 sc (*UK dc*) 3 times in side sts to beginning.

Tie off the end, leaving a length of yarn around 15cm (6in) long. Use the thread to sew loose gathering stitches through the base chain. Pull up the work and form it into a circle. Sew the sides together securely.

Materials and equipment:

No. 3 crochet cotton in red and pink

Crochet hook size 3.00mm (US D-0, UK 11)

Sewing needle and thread

Bodkin or large-eyed needle for sewing the flower together

For a more subtle effect, the carnation can be worked in a single colour, as shown by the pale green version in the photograph on the right.

Scabious

Instructions:

Make 4 ch, join with a ss into a ring.

Round 1: *ss into loop, 7 ch, miss 2 ch, ss into next 5 ch*, repeat from * to * 10 more times (11 petals).

Round 2: *ss into space between petals 1 and 2 from round 1 keeping yarn behind, 6 ch, miss 2 ch, ss into next 4 ch*, repeat from * to * 10 more times, working between the petals from round 1. You should now have made 11 more petals, making 22 petals in total.

Round 3: *ss into base ch between petals 1 and 2 from round 2, 5 ch, miss 2 ch, ss into next 3 ch*, repeat from * to * 10 more times, working between the petals. You should now have made 11 more petals, making 33 petals in total.

Round 4: ss into base of first petal from round 3, break yarn and thread through to back of work.

Thread a needle with sewing thread and bring the thread through to the centre of the flower from the back. Thread on a bugle bead followed by a small bead, then pass the needle through the bugle bead again. Leave the thread slightly loose so that the beads are not held too tightly. Repeat for the remaining beads then secure on the back of the work with a few stitches.

Materials and equipment:

Multicoloured ribbon yarn

Crochet hook size 4.50mm (US G, UK 7)

9 red bugle beads

9 small red beads

Sewing needle or beading needle and thread

Bodkin or large-eyed needle for sewing the flower together

Attach the flower to a ribbon to make it into a pretty bracelet, as shown in the photograph on the facing page.

Black Orchid

Instructions:

Make 10 ch, ss into a ring.

Round 1: *3 ch, dtr (*UK ttr*) into ring, ttr (*UK quad tr*), 3 ch, miss 2 ch, sc (*UK dc*) into first ch, 2 ttr (*UK quad tr*), dtr (*UK ttr*), 3 ch, sc (*UK dc*) into ring*, repeat from * to * twice more, making 3 petals.

5 sc (*UK dc*) around the base ring. Press the flower.

Round 2: 2 ch, ss into centre base of petal 1, 4 ch, ss into centre base of petal 2, 4 ch, ss into centre base of petal 3, 2 ch, ss into base sp of petal 3, 5 sc (*UK dc*) in sc (*UK dc*) of base ring, 2 sc (*UK dc*) into 2 ch sp.

*sc (*UK dc*) into 4 ch sp, 3 ch, dtr (*UK ttr*), ttr (*UK quad tr*), 3 ch, miss

2 ch, sc (*UK dc*) into first ch, 2 ttr (*UK quad tr*), dtr (*UK ttr*), 3 ch, sc (*UK dc*) into 2 ch sp*, repeat from * to * to end of round.

Five petals have now been made: 3 larger petals at the back of the work and two slightly smaller petals at the front. Do not cut the yarn. Press all the petals.

Centre front petal (lip)

5 ch, ss into base of petal 4, turn.

Round 3: 2 ch, [hdc (*UK htr*), 3 dc (*UK tr*), hdc (*UK htr*)] into 5 ch sp from round 2, ss into base of petal 5.

Round 4: 4 ch, ss into base of petal 4 (push the lobe upwards to fill the gap made by 10 ch loop), turn.

Round 5: 1 ch, sc (*UK dc*), hdc (*UK htr*), 3 dc (*UK tr*), hdc (*UK htr*), sc (*UK dc*), ss into base of petal 5, turn.

Round 6: work into sts from round 5. 1 ch, miss 1 sc (*UK dc*), 2 hdc (*UK htr*), dc (*UK tr*), 3 ch, miss 2 ch, ss into ch, dc (*UK tr*), 2 hdc (*UK htr*), sc (*UK dc*), ss into base of petal 4.

Tie and fasten off the end.

Note: it is important that the lobe created in round 4 is pushed up to fill the gap. It should then be sewn in place before attaching the ribbons and beads (see below).

Cut the organza ribbon into 4 lengths and stitch them into the centre of the flower, above the lip. Cut the satin ribbon into 2 unequal lengths and attach them on top of the organza. Sew a cluster of black and clear beads in the centre of the flower.

Who says crochet and glamour don't mix? This stunning black orchid will add a touch of sophistication to any outfit.

Materials and equipment:

Black ribbon yarn

Crochet hook size 3.50mm (US E-00, UK 9)

40cm (16in) length of black organza ribbon

27cm (10¾in) length of narrow black satin ribbon

Various small black and clear beads

Sewing needle and thread

Bodkin or large-eyed needle for sewing in the ends

Orange Blossom

Instructions:

Using yellow crochet cotton, make 4 ch, join with a ss into a ring.

Round 1: 1 ch, 5 sc (*UK dc*) into ring, ss into 1 ch.

Round 2: 2 ch, 1 dc (*UK tr*) into each sc (*UK dc*), ss to join, tie off the end.

Rejoin white crochet cotton at base of work, work into sc (*UK dc*) strand.

Round 3: *6 ch, miss 1 ch, 1 sc (*UK dc*) into next ch, 1 hdc (*UK htr*) into next ch, 1 dc (*UK tr*) into next ch, 1 tr (*UK dtr*) into next ch, 1 dtr (*UK ttr*) into next ch, ss into next st of first round*, repeat from * to * 4 more times, making 5 petals in total. End in same st as join.

Tie off and sew in the ends.

Join the sewing thread to the reverse of the flower and push the needle up through the space between the yellow centre and the white ridge surrounding it. Thread on a bead and take the thread back through to the back of the work. Repeat, sewing on beads all around the yellow flower centre.

Materials and equipment:

No. 3 crochet cotton in yellow and white

Crochet hook size 2.50mm (US B-1, UK 13)

Various small orange beads

Sewing needle and orange thread

Bodkin or large-eyed needle for sewing in the ends

These pretty little flowers look great on accessories around the home – try them on hanging hearts, napkin rings, jewellery boxes and notebooks, for example, to add that personal touch.

Aquilegia

Instructions:

Centre

With 3.00mm (US D-0, UK 11) hook and yellow thread, make a magic ring (see below, left), 5 sc (UK dc) into centre, join with ss into 1st sc (UK dc), cut yarn.

Inner petals

With white thread *ss into sc (UK dc) sp, 2 ch, 2 dc (UK tr), 2 ch, ss into next sc (UK dc), ss* repeat into each sc (UK dc) sp 4 more times (5 petals). Next work into the back of the petal. Insert hook through centre back 2 dc (UK tr) loop of first inner petal, *ss, 1 ch, ss *hook through the back on next inner petal 2 dc (UK tr) loops, continuing working at back of petals until you have five 1 ch loops. Cut yarn.

Outer petals

Change to 2.50mm (US B-1, UK 13) hook and with blue stranded cotton, work into 1 ch loops.

Row 1: *ss, 3 ch, 1 tr (UK dtr), 2 ch, ss into 1 st ch, 1tr (UK dtr), 3 ch, ss into next 1 ch sp* repeat 4 more times. (5 petals). Cut yarn. Sew in the ends securely.

Materials and equipment

Crochet hooks sizes 2.50mm (US B-1, UK 13) and 3.00mm (US D-0, UK 11)

Crochet cotton perle in yellow and white

Stranded cotton embroidery thread in cornflower blue

Sewing needle with large eye

To make a magic ring

Wrap yarn around index and middle fingers, making sure you leave a length of 6–8cm (2³⁄₈–3¼in), forming a ring. Holding both strands of yarn where they overlap, push the working yarn behind the ring between your fingers, towards you, pull this loop, ch 1 and start the following pattern.

These mini flowers are also known as Granny's Bonnet. They would look lovely sewn securely on to a baby's blanket, or could be used to decorate a hair clip or purse.

Sweet Peas

Instructions:

Outer petals

With 2.50mm (US B-1, UK 13) hook and pink make a 4 ch, ss into 1st ch to form loop.

Round 1: 1 ch, 10 sc (UK dc) into loop, ss into 1 st ch.

Round 2: 1 ch, 1 sc (UK dc) into each of next 3 sc (UK dc), 2 dc (UK tr) into next 4 sc (UK dc), 1 sc (UK dc) into next 3 sc (UK dc), ss into 1 ch.

Round 3: 1 ch, 1sc (UK dc) into each of next 3 sc (UK dc), 2 hdc (UK htr) into next 8 dc (UK tr) 1 sc (UK dc) into next 3 sc (UK dc), ss into 1 ch.

Round 4: 1 ch, 1sc (UK dc) into each of next 3 sc (UK dc), 2 hdc (UK htr) into next 16 hdc (UK htr), 1 sc (UK dc) into next 3 sc (UK dc), ss into 1 ch.

For plain petal use Round 5, or for frilled petal use Rounds 5 and 6.

Round 5: 1 ch, 1 sc (UK dc) into next 3 sc (UK dc), 2 dc (UK tr) into next 32 hdc (UK htr), 1sc (UK dc) into next 3 sc (UK dc).

Round 6: *2 ch, ss* into 3 sc (UK dc), all dc (UK tr) and last 3 sc (UK dc).

Inner petals

Using 2.00mm (US B-1, UK 14) hook and pink, make a 3 ch, ss into 1 st ch to form loop.

Round 1: 2 ch, 4 dc (UK tr), 2 ch, ss, 2 ch, 4 dc (UK tr), 2 ch all into loop.

Round 2: ss then sc (UK dc) into 2 ch sp, sc (UK dc) into dc (UK tr), dc (UK tr) into next 3 dc (UK tr), 2 dc (UK tr) then sc (UK dc) into 2 ch sp, ss into loop, sc (UK dc) then 2 dc (UK tr) into 2 ch sp, dc (UK tr) into next 3 dc (UK tr),sc (UK dc) into 2 ch sp, ss into loop, ss into sc (UK dc) at beginning of round.

Round 3: sc (UK dc) into next sc (UK dc), dc (UK tr) into next dc (UK tr), 2 dc (UK tr) into next 5 dc (UK tr), sc (UK dc) into sc (UK dc). Ss into loop, sc (UK dc) into sc (UK dc), 2 dc (UK tr) into next 5 dc (UK tr), sc (UK dc) into sc (UK dc), ss into 1st sc (UK dc).

To make up

Lay inner petal on to outer petal, and place the centre loop from the inner petal slightly above the loop of the outer petal. Using end threads, sew together at the loop points, fold the bottom of the outer petal up and stitch together above the inner petal. Pinch the centre bottom of the outer petal to create a small fold, and stitch together. Sew in any thread ends neatly. Fold the top of the outer petal back. Add a stem by pushing florist wire through the centre of the inner petal, bend it and push it back through, trapping a few, stitches, then twist the florist wire together to secure it. Wrap green yarn over the wire.

This little spray of sweet peas makes a great buttonhole decoration, either for a dressy occasion or just on your denims!

Materials and equipment:

Crochet hooks sizes 2.50mm (US B-1, UK 13) and 2.00mm (US B-1, UK 14)

Pink crochet cotton

Florist wire 28 gauge

Green yarn

Sewing needle with large eye

Red Anemone

Instructions:

With the size 2.50mm (US B-1, UK 13) hook and black, make 10 ch, join with ss in first ch to form a ring.

Then make 7 petals off ring as follows:

Row 1: 4 sc (*UK dc*) into centre ring, turn.

Row 2: 1 ch, 1sc (*UK dc*) into next 4 sc (*UK dc*), turn, cut black yarn.

Row 3: join in white, 1 ch, 2 SC (*UK dc*) into next sc (*UK dc*), 1 sc (*UK dc*) into next 3 sc (*UK dc*), 2 sc (*UK dc*) into last sc (*UK dc*), turn.

Row 4: 1 ch, 2 sc (*UK dc*) into next sc (*UK dc*), 1 sc (*UK dc*) into next 5 sc (*UK dc*), 2 sc (*UK dc*) into next sc (*UK dc*), turn, cut white yarn.

Row 5: join in red, 1 ch, 2 sc (*UK dc*) into next sc (*UK dc*), 1 sc (*UK dc*) into next 7 sc (*UK dc*), 2 sc (*UK dc*) into next sc (*UK dc*), turn.

Row 6: 1 ch, 1 sc (*UK dc*) into next 11 sc (*UK dc*), turn.

Rows 7–11: repeat row 6.

Row 11: ss, sc (*UK dc*), hdc (*UK htr*), dc (*UK tr*), 2 tr (*UK dtr*), dtr (*UK ttr*), 2 tr (*UK dtr*), dc (*UK tr*), hdc (*UK htr*), sc (*UK dc*), ss.

Work using above pattern into centre ring until 7 petals are made.

To make up

Join each petal by first sewing the black parts together, leave as many loose ends of the black as possible as these will be pulled through the centre ring. Join the white and red sections of the petals together, tying off the ends neatly at the back of the work. Sew in any loose ends securely. Add more loose black threads to the centre ring if required, and sew a black button into the centre ring.

Opposite
This bright anemone makes a bold statement on a hat or scarf.

Materials and equipment:

Crochet hook size 2.50mm (US B-1, UK 13)

Small amount of black yarn

White crochet cotton

Red crochet cotton

Black button

Sewing needle with large eye

Lisianthus

Instructions:

Flower

With size 3mm (US D-0, UK 11) hook and white, make 6 ch, join with ss in first ch to form a ring.

Row 1: miss 2 ch, starting in 3rd ch from hook, 1 sc (*UK dc*) into next 4 ch, turn.

Row 2: 1 ch, 2 sc (*UK dc*) into each of next 2 sc (*UK dc*), miss sc (*UK dc*), 1 sc (*UK dc*) into last sc (*UK dc*), turn.

Row 3: 1 ch, 1 sc (*UK dc*) into next 5 sc (*UK dc*), turn.

Row 4: 1 ch, 1 sc (*UK dc*) into next 5 sc (*UK dc*), turn.

Row 5: 1 ch, 2 sc (*UK dc*) into each of next 4 sc (*UK dc*), 1 sc (*UK dc*) into last sc (*UK dc*), turn.

Row 6 to 9: 1 ch, 1 sc (*UK dc*) into next 9 sc (*UK dc*), turn.

Row 10: bring in pink, using both white and pink yarns together 1 ch, 1 sc (*UK dc*) into next 9 sc (*UK dc*), turn.

Row 11: using pink only, 1 ch, 1 sc (*UK dc*) into next 9 sc (*UK dc*), turn.

Row 12: 1 ch, 1 sc (*UK dc*), 1 hdc (*UK htr*), 1 hdc (*UK htr*), 3 dc (*UK tr*), 1 hdc (*UK htr*), 1 hdc (*UK htr*), 1 sc (*UK dc*), ss.

Make 5 petals.

Stamen

With 2mm (US B-1, UK 14) hook, make a 5 ch, miss 2 ch, 1 sc (*UK dc*) into next 3 sc (*UK dc*), cut and leave 15cm (6in) length.

Make 3 stamen.

To make up

Sew in loose pink thread ends neatly at the back of the work. Sew loose white threads along the side of the petal, leaving a length of thread for sewing petals together.

Cut a 30cm (11¾in) length of green yarn, pinch all three stamen together and wrap this yarn around the loose threads, then tie and cut it. Take one petal, wrap it round the bottom of the of stamens and sew it in place. Take the next petal, wrap it round the first and sew them together at the base. Continue with the next three petals, joining the bottom edges and lower 2cm (¾in).

Wrap green thread around all loose ends securely, tie and cut.

Materials and equipment:

Crochet hooks sizes 2.00mm (US B-1, UK 14) and 3.00mm (US D-0, UK 11)

White crochet cotton

Pink crochet cotton

Small amount of green yarn

Sewing needle

Stemmed flowers like these
make excellent buttonholes,
but also look beautiful as
decorations around the house.

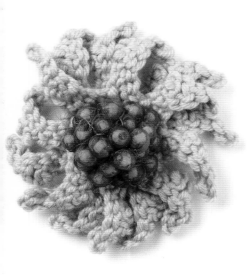

Echinacea

Instructions:

With 3.50mm (US E-00, UK 9) hook make a 5 ch, ss through 1 st ch to form ring.

Round 1: ch 3, 15 dc (UK tr) into ring, join with ss.

Round 2: *ss into back dc (*UK tr*), ch 9, work into back of ch as follows – miss 2 ch, ss into next ch, 1 sc (*UK dc*) into next 2 ch, 1 dc (*UK tr*) into next 2 ch, 1 sc (*UK dc*) into next 2 ch, ss into next back dc (*UK tr*)* repeat 7 more times (8 petals).

Round 3: *ss into front dc (*UK tr*) between round 1 petals, ch 9, miss 2 ch, ss into next ch, 1 sc (*UK dc*) into next 2 ch, 1 dc (*UK tr*) into next 2 ch, 1 sc (*UK dc*) into next 2 ch, ss into next back dc (*UK tr*)* repeat 7 more times (8 petals).

Centre

Using the sheer fabric, fold and stitch along its length to form a tube. Thread beads on to thread, leaving a good length of thread each end. Feed the length of beads though the fabric tube and sew one end of the bead thread to the edge of the fabric tube. Carefully wrap the beads and fabric into a circle, securing each bead as you go, make sure the cut edge of the fabric is facing the same way, as this will be used to secure the centre through the middle of the petals.

Turn the petals over (so they are 'hanging' downwards. Place the centre of the beads on to the centre of the crochet petals and sew them together.

Materials and equipment:

Crochet hook size 3.50mm (US E-00, UK 9)

Gold baby yarn, fingering (UK 4 ply)

Sheer brown fabric, 30 x 3cm (11¾ x 1¼in)

20 x 4mm (³/₁₆in) yellow beads

Rust-coloured thread

Beading and sewing needles

This beautiful echinacea flower will look lovely on a coat, scarf or bag.

Lobelia

Instructions:

With 2.50mm (US B-1, UK 13) hook and deep purple crochet cotton perle, make 4 ch, ss through ch 1 to form a ring.

Round 1: Working into loop *2 ch, 1 dc (*UK tr*), 1 tr (*UK dtr*), 1 dc (*UK tr*), 2 ch, ss* repeat twice more (forms 3 petals) then 2 ch, *1 dc (*UK tr*), 2 ch, ss into 1 ch (to form picot st) 1 dc (*UK tr*), 2 ch, ss* repeat to form 2 pointed petals) 5 petals in total.

ss, break yarn, stitch loose end into flower.

With white yarn form a double cross, using the centre loop as cross-over point.

Using black yarn, create the small detail knot in the centre of the flower as follows: ch 3, miss 2, sc (*UK dc*), turn, sc (*UK dc*) into sc (*UK dc*), tie off ends.

Materials and equipment:

Crochet hook size 2.50mm (US B-1, UK 13)

Deep purple crochet cotton perle

Small amounts of white and black yarn

Sewing needle

Opposite

These deep purple flowers will add an exotic finishing touch to your clothes, accessories or home.

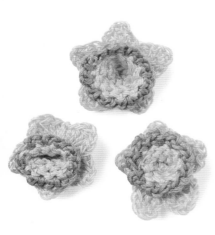

Narcissus

Instructions:

Petals

With size 2.50mm (US B-1, UK 13) hook and yellow, make 10 ch, join with ss in first ch to form a ring.

*1 sc (*UK dc*), 2 dc (*UK tr*), 1ch, 1 tr (*UK dtr*), 1 ch, 2 dc (*UK tr*), 1 sc (*UK dc*)* into ring 5 times, ss into 1 st sc (*UK dc*).

Trumpet

Make a magic ring (see page 110), ch 1 and 4 sc (*UK dc*) into centre, join with ss.

Round 1: ch 1 *2 sc (*UK dc*) in next stitch, sc (*UK dc*), * repeat once, join with ss.

Round 2: ch 1, 1 sc (*UK dc*) into each sc (*UK dc*), join with ss. (6sts)

Round 3: Repeat Round 2.

Round 4: Repeat Round 2, bring in orange thread.

Round 5: ch 1, 1 sc (*UK dc*) into base sc (*UK dc*) of ch, *ss, 1 ch, sc (*UK dc*) into next sc (*UK dc*)* repeat to last sc (*UK dc*), ss to join.

To make up

Place the trumpet inside the centre of the petals and sew together.

Materials and equipment:

Crochet hook size 2.50mm (US B-1, UK 13)

Yellow crochet cotton, use double

Small amount of orange yarn

Sewing needle and yellow thread

Narcissi have such associations of spring. Use them to decorate the table for a spring party, or to cheer up your winter clothes.

Auricula in pot

Instructions:

Flowers

Using 2.50mm (US B-1, UK 13) hook and yellow, make a magic ring (see page 110).

Round 1: 8 sc (*UK dc*) into ring.

Round 2: With lime, join with ss, 1 ch, 2 sc (*UK dc*) into next 8 sc (*UK dc*).

Round 3: With red, join with ss into 1ch sp, *ss into next sc (*UK dc*), 2 ch, dc (*UK tr*) into same sc (*UK dc*), 2 tr (*UK dtr*) into next sc (*UK dc*), 1 dc (*UK tr*), 2 ch, ss into next sc (*UK dc*),* repeat 4 more times (5 petals) ss into next sc (*UK dc*), tie off end, leave length for sewing in.

Make 14 flowers.

Flower pot

With 3.50mm (US E-00, UK 9) hook and cream dishcloth yarn, make a magic ring (see page 110).

Round 1: 9 sc (*UK dc*) into ring join with ss.

Round 2: 3 ch, *2 dc (*UK tr*) into sc (*UK dc*), 1 dc (*UK tr*) into sc (UK dc)* repeat 3 more times, 2 dc (*UK tr*) into last sc (*UK dc*), join with ss.

Round 3: 3 ch, 2 dc (*UK tr*), into all dc (*UK tr*), join with ss.

Round 4: 3 ch, *dc (*UK tr*) into next 4 dc (*UK tr*), 2 dc (*UK tr*) into next dc (*UK tr*)* repeat from * to last 2 dc (*UK tr*), 2 dc (*UK tr*) join with ss.

Round 5: 2 ch hdc (*UK htr*) into back loop of all dc (*UK tr*), join with ss.

Round 6: 3 ch, dc (*UK tr*) into all hdc (*UK htr*), join with ss.

Round 7: 3 ch, * dc (*UK tr*) into next 5 dc (*UK tr*), miss dc (*UK tr*)* repeat 6 more times, dc (*UK tr*) into next 5 dc (*UK tr*), join with ss.

Rounds 8–11: 3 ch, dc (*UK tr*) into all dc (*UK tr*), join with ss.

Round 12: Change to 4.00mm (US G-6, UK 8) hook, turn, 3 ch, 2 tr (*UK dtr*) into each dc (*UK tr*) sp, 1 tr (*UK dtr*) into base of 3 ch, join into 3rd ch with ss, turn.

Round 13: Change to 3.50mm (US E-00, UK 9) hook, 2 ch, *1 dc (*UK tr*), miss tr (*UK dtr*) * repeat from * to * ss into 2 ch sp.

Round 14: Repeat round 13.

Round 15: 1 ch, 1sc (*UK dc*) into all dc (*UK tr*), join with ss.

Round 16: 1 ch, *1 tr (*UK dtr*) into each of next 4 sc (*UK dc*), miss tr (*UK dtr*)* repeat from * to end, ss into 2 ch, tie off.

Materials and equipment:

Crochet hooks sizes 2.50mm (US B-1, UK 13), 3.50mm (US E-00, UK 9) and 4.00mm (US G-6, UK 8)

Crochet cotton perle in yellow, lime and red

Cream dishcloth yarn

Green chunky (12 ply) yarn

Florist wire in 18 and 28 gauge and pliers for cutting

Rice

Freezer bag with tie top

Circle of fabric

Plastic flower pot

Glue gun (optional)

Masking tape

Wool oddments for embroidery

Crewel needle for embroidery

Leaves

Using green chunky yarn, make a 8 ch, ss through ch 1 to form loop.

Round 1: *ch 8, 3 sc (*UK dc*)* into ring, repeat 5 more times, ss into 1st ch (6 leaves).

Round 2: *sc (*UK dc*), 2 dc (*UK tr*), tr (*UK dtr*), dc (*UK tr*), 2 ch, ss into 1st ch, dc (*UK tr*), tr (*UK dtr*), 2 dc (*UK tr*), sc (*UK dc*) into next 8 ch sp, sc (*UK dc*) into 1 ch* sc (*UK dc*) into 2nd of 3 sc (*UK dc*) working into each 8 ch sp, from * to * ss into 1st sc (*UK dc*), tie off for the last time.

Making up

Draw a circle 4cm (1½in) larger in diameter than the top of the flower pot on to the back of the fabric and cut it out. Cover the flower pot with the the crocheted cover. Place the freezer bag in the flowerpot with the top hanging over the edges, fill to 1cm (³⁄₈in) below the top of the flower pot with rice and tie securely.

Cut fourteen 15cm (6in) lengths of thin florist wire, thread both ends of a wire through the centre of a flower from front to back, with one end protruding by 2cm (¾in) and the other end by 13cm (5in), twist the wire ends together behind the flower to make a stem and clamp the short ends of wire with pliers to create a neat join. Repeat for all fourteen flowers. Wrap green yarn around each stem leaving 5cm (2in) unwrapped at the base. Take the thicker florist wire, bend it in half and form a loop at the bend by twisting it. Thread the fourteen stems though the loop, twisting each one so it sits on top of the bent thick wire, which makes the main stem. Wrap green yarn around the top 6cm (2½in) of thick wire, weaving the yarn between the 1 fourteen flower stems to secure it, and tie off.

Place the fabric circle over the top of the flower pot, pushing the excess fabric down the inside of the pot. For extra strength, glue around the inside edges. Push the thick wire stem through the centre circle of the leaves. Place the leaves on top of the flower pot and push the end of the thick wire stem into the rice (if you find it difficult to push wire through fabric, make a small slit and feed wire through). Using masking tape, attach the stems securely to the bag of rice. Sew the end of each leaf to the the dishcloth yarn flower pot cover.

Embroider a lazy daisy stitch design of flowers and stems on to the front of the flower pot cover.

Opposite

These stunning auriculas will brighten your home all year round, and will not need watering! You can experiment with making a pot of some of the other flowers in this book and make someone a beautiful gift that will never wilt.

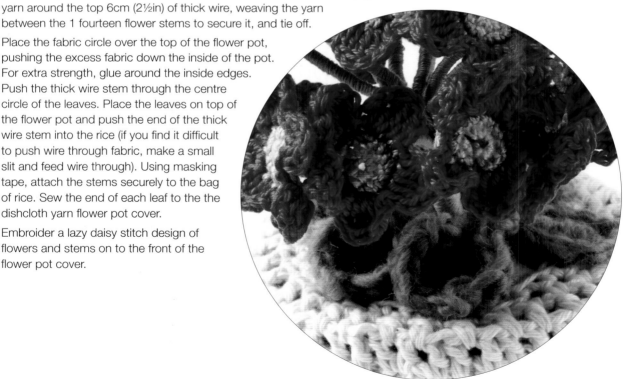